A TELL OF TWO WARS

The wars came to be more than rumors; unexpected,
unplanned, undeclared, unwanted, and unpopular.

I.G.

AuthorHouse™ LLC
1663 Liberty Drive
Bloomington, IN 47403
www.authorhouse.com
Phone: 1-800-839-8640

Published by AuthorHouse   02/28/2014

ISBN: 978-1-4918-6896-6 (sc)
ISBN: 978-1-4918-6897-3 (e)

Library of Congress Control Number: 2014903613

CHAPTER 1

THE FINAL REQUEST

The two men had been riding in silence as the car pulled up to a dull, gray and bleak-looking building. The driver spoke up as they got out of the car, "Sir, I know they searched you at the main building, but you will have to undergo a strip search before you can see anyone here." The door slowly opened, both men entered under the watchful eyes of the guards in the control room. "Open one," the guard on the other side of a steel and bulletproof glass commanded. Both stepped in, the escort guard first then the visitor. "Empty your pockets, take your belt shoes and pants off." As the visitor disrobed the guard went through each article, handing them back upon thorough examination. "He's clean;" the officer turned to the control room operator. "Roll two." The gate buzzed open and they stepped out. The escort led the visitor down a long corridor lined with cameras, like big brother watching their every move.

I.G.

"I'll take you to the visitation staging area where they will bring him in." The man nodded his approval as a puzzled look crossed his face. He couldn't help wondering why he had been summoned to this place so suddenly at the request of a person whom he didn't even know. He had lectured, done workshops, toured, and even volunteered at many facilities such as this one all over the country. Some of the places he had been were like dungeons and houses of horrors, but this place gave him an eerie feeling that was chilling to the bone.

At the end of the corridor a stone-faced guard stood at attention. In the entrance way of an empty room, which only housed a table and two chairs on either side, the escort stopped at the doorway motioning for him to enter alone. The iron-gate clanged shut behind him. It seemed an eternity, as he sat waiting for his host, he heard the clinking of chains getting closer and closer; it reminded him of a movie he had seen in which the goats of Christmas past came to visit a man whose life was about to make a sudden and unexpected change. Suddenly a heavy door on the other side of the room slowly opened. An athletic built chain-laden man with salt and pepper hair entered the room. The guard unshackled his hands. The prisoner asked the guard for a cigarette, sat down and spoke slowly. "You don't know me. My name is Casey Johnson. Twenty-five years ago your father and I played ball on opposing teams in high school.

After graduation we were drafted into the service together. When we went to Viet Nam, there were three of us from the same neighborhood, your father, Sargent Carter, and I made a pact to watch each other's back during the war. Your dad didn't change much from the way he was in high school. But something inside of me died the day our platoon encountered a V.C held village on one of our patrols.

His mind began to drift back. "We were in the Central Highlands, known as the 'Killing Zone' we combed the village looking for any signs of the enemy, secret hiding places or tunnels weapons, clothing and food. All of a sudden shots rang out from nowhere. One of the men hollered, "It's an ambush! Hit the deck!" All hell broke loose and things got real crazy as the guys in our platoon starting firing into the huts. Men women and children, most of them were innocent," his head dropped. "We turned them all into jelly. I can still see those eyes with terror and fear, staring at me in the middle of the night." He stopped, remorse in his voice, he then continued. "Your father withdrew from the rest of us and stayed by himself after that. It hurt him deeply. Killing wasn't part of his makeup, because he wasn't cut like that. But a few of the other guys and I took the macho approach to justify that was the reason for us being there, and after that incident, the taking of human life became easier. We used drugs more and more to ease the pain and cover up our true feelings. I was also involved in black marketing and stealing anything I could get my hands on. I signed up for another tour it got so good to me. It was right after I started my second tour that I heard about your father being killed in Da Nang." Casey wiped his eyes, looking solemn. "It was the first time since the age of twelve that I cried. We were only kids upon entering the service and they made killers out of us. They drilled into us destroy or be destroyed. We became professional killers our duty in those jungles was search and destroy and add onto the body count. Those emotions can't just be turned off like a light switch. "It was on my R&R (rest and recuperation), in Bangkok Thailand that I found the real secret or meaning behind the war that so many of my homes like your father had died for. It was then I made up in my mind to get mine before my number was up.

A serious expression came across his face. "Did you know Viet Nam, Laos, and Thailand along with Afghanistan and Burma make up the nations that are known as the Golden Triangle; which are the regions and main source of Opium and Heroin production in the world? The Opium and Heroin is shipped to various locations in North Thailand down to Bangkok. The drugs were at first brought down trails by caravans of mule's oxen, or small vehicles or by boat by way of the Macon Delta into Thailand until the war started to escalate and it became increasingly dangerous for the communist, either seizing or stopping the flow. There was this guy an Ex-GI, like the one in Apocalypse Now, who was a former military man working with certain elements of the C.I.A who were training tribe's man in Laos, along with what was then military advisers. He told me they helped a Laotian General use some C.I.A's Air America planes, arms and money for the tribe's man in exchange for their Opium and Heroin to transport them down the Ho Chi Men trail through parts of North Viet Nam into Thailand then to military bases in South Viet Nam. The MOGE or Myanmar Oil and Gas Co. were the main channel for laundering revenues of Heroin production a sweet operation that ran like clock-work. It was under certain elements of the C.I.A's direction and control that a secret Army of Royal Lao's fighters were formed to ensure its safe passage.

When I was in Bangkok I met an ex-master sergeant who owned a popular night club in the heart of the city which became the headquarters where connections were formed and covert plots were put together. He got me to volunteer for a unit called the 'Head Hunters' which was a special opts detachment of a select few regular and former military person who took no prisoners and wore charm necklaces made out of human ears, eyes, noses, tongs, pennies and even scalps. We got paid extra by the amount of body parts that were collected. We were part of what was called *Steel Tiger* that was assigned to protect U.S. and C.I.A's airstrips. The entire operation known as (iron arc) made sure all those C-1 30 transport cargo planes were protected. Our military objective was to let nothing happened to the shipments coming from Laos through Thailand by whatever means that deemed necessary. A University of Georgia professor, after much resource and investigation, came to the conclusion that the C.I.A.'s led covert action in Laos was the largest operation in the history of the agency. Certain agents assisted illicit drug activities of the local leaders in nations like Laos, Thailand, and of course Viet Nam in exchange for cooperation in the war effort against communism. Someone came up with the idea to use the Heroin and Opium connection that had been forged by the (French Connection) and possibly use it for the rebellion in the U.S. inner city streets." Danny looked the prisoner up and down with a doubtful puzzled disdained smirk. The man continued "Don't let my present state of being fool you, all this information although top-secret but true."

How much do you know about the history of up and coming small nations gaining power and control over bigger and stronger Empires, and doing it by any means necessary? A small Island country like England came to rule an Empire where the sun never set. In order to subdue a country large as China they needed to waged what was called the Opium Wars, not one but two. Opium and Heroin was such a profitable and potent weapon that they were able to boast their ailing economy while destroying the will and resistance of the Chinese by simply turning the population into drug addicts. A sinister plan was like killing two birds with one stone. The government of England sent their war-ships and troops into China with Opium grown in the fields of Burma and Afghanistan, which at that time was under their 'colony rule' and part of India (the jewel of the British Empire). What worked for the British would be tried out by some gung ho C.I.A. operatives, to subdue what J. Eager Hoover himself called the greatest threat to America's security, civil unrest or what the world came to know as the Civil Rights Movement. It was to blame, by some elements of society, as the anti-social struggle and vehicle that brought about all the militant and radical groups (Black Panthers, Wheatear Man etc.) Many in government and the military felt that they were standing up for America and what this country stood for by an all-out war on these rouge radical and militant factions. We can't forget how serious this was back then many groups were calling for a 'Revolution' to over-throw the present American System and give back 'power to the people' and they dam near pulled it off. To stop it, top level officials like that 'Bull Dog' who headed up the F.B.I along with ranking military persons plotted to eliminate the threat over there and over here.

That Sargent who owned a night club in Bangkok was an important link in the chain because he had a connection with the Kuomintang Opium smuggling operation, which were forces loyal to General Chiang Kai Shek, still fighting communism. The C.I.A would use places where American G.I.s hung out to make their covert deals. The drugs were smuggled from Burma to Bangkok. There they used the C.I.A's Air-America along with the military transport plane flying them to U.S. Army bases like Fort Bragg where those who were in on the secret smuggling operation would distribute them to East and West Coast cities. The 'American Gangster' selling what was called 'blue magic' in Harlem had his connection through that Sargent. The C.I.A knew what he was doing and he found out something about their operation, neither interfered with the other because both were in the same business helping to destroy the Inner cities while making great profits." Danny gave the man a look like he was listening to a delusional mad man.

"Those are some serious allegations, because it seems to me you are just making up all the non-sense to blame someone else or possibly justify what you have done. Casey contoured. "Look I am not saying the war was fought solely for the purpose of a government cover-up of our C.I.A's drug smuggling operation. I believe it did start as a result of the U.S. trying to flex its muscles in Southeast Asia to make sure the Chinese and Russians didn't get a foot hold in Viet Nam like they tried to in Korea. Our military had convinced the President and the government that this one would be over quickly and we would spank their asses and save our face at the same time. Of course it didn't work out like that and as the war dragged on so did the outrage on college campuses and protest, in the streets of cities like Newark, Chicago, Detroit, L.A., and after Dr. King's death Washington D.C. itself was ablaze with the fire of rebellion. Power is as addictive as any drug, and those that have it will do anything to keep it. Men in control became desperate because they saw themselves being under attack in the Viet Nam jungles and in the jungles of America's inner city streets we could say on two wars on two fronts. They even had to send troops just back from Viet Nam into the line of fire to war zone 'Detroit.'

The top priority became our big cities; top government officials knew it had to win the streets back. All is fair in love and war and people had no love lost for neither soldiers nor the system that was in power. The British had conquered China a nation of a billion people by putting out the fire of resistance by their use of Opium. Certain elements of the C.I.A convinced leading government officials in the late 1960's that the only way to prevent a Revolution in America was to fight a covert (Contelpro) a secret war. They couldn't keep using troops to fight in U.S. cities. It was simple to use a weapon that the victims would come to depend on, want it more than anything else, do anything to get it even if it meant turning against anyone to have it (brother against brother, son against father and mothers forgetting their own children), war was literality being waged against a part of society without their knowledge. There was no such thing as a war on drugs, because the only war was for the power to control those who had control over the enormous profits that came with it. What was happening over in Viet Nam became a side show; the drug pipeline to the U.S. being kept open was the biggest show in town." Danny slid his chair all the way back becoming emerged in deep thought while shaking his head. "That's a hell of a story which could shine a different light on what my father fought and died for." The dead serious convict leaned forward. "True that, because it is true, I know because I was involved with those individuals who were directly in it up to their necks. They trusted me I became privy to all this secretly sensitive information; I became one of them an assassin, killer, and bounty hunter on the government's payroll." Danny gave the man a hard look. "So what do you want from me, I'm not a pastor or priest to hear your confession, nor can I put it in print because I am not a reporter either."

The hardened criminal became somber with a look of remorse in his eyes. "This ant about me, I'm not making no excuses or putting any blame on anyone else for what I have done. I am going to pay for my sins in this life and the hear-after." Dropping his head he spoke quietly. "I have a son the result of a relationship with a woman that I turned onto drugs, then a life of crime after I discharged from the

Military. And like Bonnie and Clyde we went from state robbing, stealing, and sticking up everyone and thing we could. Because of that life style we spent more time behind bars that with the boy, he went from house to house. She in a nursing home now after having her legs amputated from drug abuse. I haven't been in the boy's life since he was three, and he's only seen me three or four times in the thirteen years I've been here. The boy was physically and sexually abused while in one of those foster homes. I was here and his mother was there, so the kid grew up alone, resentful, with anger and bitterness his only companions. Children deserve to have one parent there for them. Our son had nobody.

It is said that the sins of the father enter in upon the son. And now my sixteen year old teen-age boy is in trouble. They want to take him out of the juvenile system so they can try him as an adult. I've been praying every-night that someway, somehow, god would make a-way or send someone to help me with my son so he could be spared this. I don't want him to start, spend and possibly end his life the way I have. I've been following you in the papers and on television sense you left college and went to the Olympic Games where you won two gold medals becoming a hero and role model to all the youth of this country. And in-stead of trying to get rich advertising gym shoes, that most of the kids in the inner cities couldn't afford, you and a priest help to establish not only a home for at risk teens but like Father Flannigan did at Boy's Town, you and your partners founded a community for all of the regardless of color, religion, lack of religion, gender or sexual preference, the welcome mat was for them all. The background you came from was hard and cruel, but my friend's son endured and overcame. Yours has been such a positive impact on so many kids like my son. The boy isn't bad. He's just lost, confused and alone. He's at that fork in the road of life and just needs somebody to show him the right direction. The news media says you have persuaded some judges to send borderline youths to your community as an alternative to jail. With me for a father and some bad breaks, God knows he deserves all the help he can get. Neither you nor my son has had a chance to know your fathers." The hardened convict's eyes welled with tears. Putting his hands together as if attempting to pray, he said "You're my last hope Danny Brown. Please help me save my son, for me and your father's friendship.

He could see the desperation and fear in the man's eyes and it moved him that this convict would make this his last request. "I'll do what I can to help your son." Danny pledged. It was the first time that joy was shown in the prisoner's face, as he thanked Danny from the bottom of his heart. "My appeal lawyers will tell you where he is and any other details about the boy's life that you wish to know. One of the guards walked over, leaned close and spoke to Casey. He nodded; "My time is up, Danny. Besides, they've got my seven-course meal waiting. This is the only time I can get what I want and as much as I want to eat." He stood up. "I see your father in you. He was a good man and a good friend. God bless you.

The officer led the shackled man out of the room, closing the heavy door behind. Later, as he drove down the highway, he turned on the evening news. The newscaster's voice blared. "At six o'clock this evening, time and thirteen years of endless appeals ran out for Casey Johnson. Mr. Johnson, a Viet Nam war hero, who had been convicted of killing a security guard and manager in a daring jewelry store robbery, was put to death by lethal injection this evening. He and his lawyers were hoping the governor would intervene and make a last minute call, granting him a stay of execution." Danny turned the radio off. A teardrop ran down his cheek as he thought about Casey and his father whom he never knew. He made up his mind right then and there he would do everything in his power to make sure that his father's friend final request was granted.

It turned out that Casey's son had been a part of this gang of youth in Detroit known then as Y.B.I, which had been organized by older dope men who saw the profit value in hiring under aged youth to sell their product. They knew that it would be hard to prosecute juveniles for any major crimes and they also knew that the great pool of uneducated, disillusioned, black males was endless in the inner city streets of Detroit. Young Boys Incorporated as they were called were an extremely brutal, ambitious, and well organized that was the first Afro-American drug cartel in the United States. Their main objective was to use minors as heroin (later crack cocaine) carries that took care of business fast, but were extremely deadly if their turf was violated. They started out on the North West side of Detroit and were headquartered at a bar on Dexter Av. Big Boy and W.W two of the founders drug empire spread as far East as Cleveland, Philly, D.C, New York, and even into Boston which became one of its biggest recruiters on the East Coast. This really got Danny's interest when he heard about the Boston connection he immediately thought that his cousin Thomas could possibly have been linked to such a wide reaching drug ring, along with Casey's son, possibly both working for the same cartel.

After all it was the 'Three Amigos' from Boston that took over the running of the 'Organization' after the Detroit leadership went to Federal Prison. At that time that Crack Cocaine hit the inner city streets of American totally destroying the fragile communities while making drug organizations like Y.B.I rich beyond their wildest imaginations turning brother against brother, and mother against daughter. When one of the original founders from Detroit was released from prison wanting control back he is said to be the one who had one a 'Three Amigo's' gun down in the "Voices" Bentley car that he was sitting in with her hubby. Danny was completely drawn in when he found out that Y.B.I was the model that influenced drug gangs nationally during the 1980's. All the things that his Uncle (Thomas dad) had predicted over a decade ago had now come so vividly to pass.

Casey's son was being held in Juvenile while his case had been consider to be turned over to the adult courts. The Judicial System had grown wiry of some many youth getting away with grownup violent crimes until they felt a message had to be sent so that a lesson could be learned. He knew nothing of the boy's crimes what had happened nor was the part the teen played in it, all he knew that he had made his father a promise and would do his best to see it through.

Danny had a letter of introduction from Casey's layers to a Junín ale case manager that had worked with his son. He called to get a meeting at his office in Detroit for 10: AM that next morning. The case worker had seen thousands of boys come through the system, with two few turning their lives around. Mr. Davis always held out hope. After exchanging greetings and pleasantries, Mr. Davis leaned back in his chair. "So you are the same Danny Brown that won the gold medals in the Olympic Games, and then came back to the U.S to help set up your own Boy's Town." Danny not wanting to take all the credit humbly answered. "I had made a promise to some people that are no longer with us to be a part of the solution not the problem This is the 1990's and our young men and women need a helping hand if we are to make it in the next century." "So what is your interest in this young man?" Danny put his hand on his chin smiling slightly. "His father was one of the people I made the promise to." This Mr. Davis countered. "Is that the only reason?" He leaned forward exclaiming "My cousin was 17 when he got killed committing a robbery. "Oh! Really." "Yes but that ant all he was the leader of a gang called the 'Chili Mack's' that dealt drugs in Boston's worst projects." Mr. Davis reared back with a wide grin. "The Chili Mack's, well they were organized in Detroit on the North-end and you say your cousin was the leader of the gang in Boston?" He nodded his head. Davis thought to himself. "That's right the Y.B.I. did have the Boston connection, in fact it was their biggest and best run operation in the East.

They couldn't get into New York because of the Country Boys and the Counsel controlling the operations there, so they went to Boston and set up shop. I even heard that when Big Boy and the other drug kingpins went to jail. The three Amigos took over the operation in Boston and Detroit." Danny agreed "Yea that is the information that I got." Davis joined in. "They picked a hell of a gang to be named after." "Why! Were they violent?" The Chili Mack's became one of the most notorious, ruthless, and cruel and deadly gangs who dealt Heroin in Detroit. With a sadistically leader they called T.T. the terrible, who set one of his rivals on fire and watched him burn alive." Danny was taken aback. "That cold blooded S.O.B had everybody on the North End gripped in fear of his ass." Pausing, "That's one of the reasons Detroit got the name 'Murder Capital' The head of the drug organization was an ex-vice cop who was using his muscle, that included some rouge cops called STRESS who moonlighted as hit men for his Black Mafia, to attempt to get everyone in line with him as the Black Godfather. The most that came of it was an all—out war for control of the Drug Empire, and a lot of dead bodies all over the city. The others Phony Down, West Side gang, Black Arthur's crew, and that slim guy from Texas fought him tooth and nail until everyone was dead or in jail." "Wow!" Danny joined in "Now let me tell you what was told to me."

I went to see a prisoner the day before he was put to death, and he told me he had been a Viet Nam Vet and that he was an eye witness to when, where, and how the Heroin first hit the U. S. He said it came from this place in Southeast Asia called a Triangle." Davis injected. "You mean the 'Golden Triangle' where the Drugs were grown, processed, and shipped down the Ho Chi Min Trail, along with the Macon river delta. The same systems the U.S. forces were fighting desperately to control." Nodding in agreement Danny said. "To Thailand through Bangkok down into Viet Nam the Heroin and Opium flowed night and day. He even claimed that the C.I.A used Military Planes and bases to transport the stuff here." Mr. Davis interceded. "You mean to tell me the U.S. Military and C.I.A knew about it and if so how did he find out?" "Yes he says so, it appears that he was one of them trained for a covert operation to help transport and protect the Opium and Heroin, and that he was a part of a special elite group that made sure nothing happened to the shipment." Davis paused. "You know that gangster from Harlem used to smuggle his in the caskets of dead G. I.s, but that would only account for the dope in New York. Some-one had to have a lot more sophisticated and large an organization to bring it in to all the big cities from coast to coast; and you know what." He whispered. "Those caskets" Pausing to reflect, "With the dead soldiers and Heroin lying next to them in those caskets." Choosing his words carefully, he surmised looking into Danny's eyes. "The dope should tell us if we really think and understand what the message is saying those young boys really died for the drugs lying in those boxes with them and the final insult was that they were being used to bring a lot of that death back home."

Danny jumped right in. "Some high officials in the Government had to know because those C 1-30 and C 1-40s were military planes that had clearance and access to anywhere in the U.S. without search or seizure that means civilian and Military Airports in the good old U. S of A."

Davis got up and paced a while, then turned to Danny. "Who was this guy?" "The boy I came to see, his dad Casey Johnson's final request was to save his son from all this; but that's not all I have a selfish reason for doing this." Danny paused as he reflected. "You see my father was in Johnson's unit in Viet Nam and was killed in Da Nang the place they called the 'killing zone' I never had a chance to meet him, and only knew him by the pictures my mother had besides what she told me about him. It appears that when he got hit he was thinking about her because all they could find left of him after the attack was a picture and part of his helmet." Davis was moved by his candor. "Wow Danny I am sorry to hear that." "Thanks, but I was lucky." Ringing his hands, "The cousin I told you about who had been a gang leader, well his father was killed too; he was truly a good man who became like a dad to me.

Brother Jackson to every-body in the projects that he helped either with a kind word or deed to the needy, would talk to me and Thomas for hours on end about getting out of the traps that have set before us in order for us to get out of and avoid future snags. I remember him saying that we are like the Native Americans of the late 19th century. They no longer need people to work in the fields, so the un-educated of all ethnic groups, especial the young blacks are expendable to them today like the braves and warriors were then. It became necessary to put those remaining on a reservation to be controlled, watched, or hunted down, if they escaped. Then they decided to take the 'chosen' young kids and civilize them in the white man's ways making sure that the Native American's as a people would cease to exist." Davis had a skeptical frowned on his face. "Now what has that to do with our present problem?" "The way I see it is that the Native American stood up, and were in the way becoming a threat to the white man's Westward progress. The braves and warriors were resistant, militant, and defiant. It is in the same way that our young people along with Civil-Rights advocates are defying them today. Certain leaders in this nation knows that in order to stay competitive and on top with the world and its population getting ready to double by the end of the century and that's only a decade from now, it must advance rapidly gain more wealth, and power. It all boils down to numbers and to our leaders the only number that really counts is No.1, and if they have the rest of the world not just looking to them but competing with them, they can't afford to lose. The present day braves and warriors must be controlled for a 'New World Order' I see almost the same thing happening at the end of this century to our young people. Then, it was Westward Advancement, now it is Space and the 21's century's high Tec, advancement they can't afford to have anyone or group stand in the way of them getting to the next century." "Kind of farfetched but I see your point." Davis nodded his approval.

"I believe that is one of the reasons he was killed, after leaving Chicago he was watched and when he started teaching other children besides Thomas and my-self, they became worried. After all his money and weapon was not stolen only the hearts of his family and friends especially his son Thomas, who from the time he was twelve became known as T. Man who wasn't taking nothing off no one. And you know what I idolized him for it." "Just from that we can see how important a father is to young men." Davis exclaimed. "T. Man gave up on society at the age of twelve and I had all intentions of following him, until that fateful day. It has been too many of us that have gone down the road of no return and didn't make it back, I was lucky to have something that I cared enough about and someone who cared enough about me to help me make it out. Casey once told me that every-child deserves a chance and I just want to help his son get his."

Mr. Davis spoke matter of fatly. "A lot of these boys have hardened their hearts to everything and won't let anyone in, I know Father Flanagan felt there was no such thing as a bad boy but this is a new and entirely different breed he never dealt with. This kid is being held for armed robbery and we don't know if he was the one who had the gun or not because he didn't act alone, but he won't talk because of the culture of no snitching." Danny frowned. "What happened to the others?" "They got away and we believe they can be prosecuted as adults if we could get the youngster to identify them." Shaking his head in discuss. "This thing about not being a snitch is totally ridiculous, because too many of the real criminals are getting away. But I am going to do this I will get you a meeting with the judge that will be handling the case, and see what he can do; like you say the kid deserves a break."

Judge Evans summoned Danny to his chambers and was going over the history of him and his organization. "Um, says here that your father was killed in the Viet Nam War and that you grew up in the Projects of Boston the Roxbury district. Yet you became one of the most celebrated high school athletes in the state, winning a scholarship to college." Danny modestly injected. "Yes Your-honor it was in Track and Field at Tennessee State University." "Umami very impressive young man, because not only that but you also went to the Olympic Games and won two gold medals for your country. Then after getting married it says that you, your wife, and a minister converted an old farm into the Y.P.H. (young people's home-farm)." Sincerity in his eyes Danny said. "I was fortunate Your-Honor, I was part of a winning team of real friends, and I always had someone who believed in me, getting help along the way; I truly think that made all the difference in the world, someone was there who gave me a break." Judge Evans glanced down at the folder over his glasses. "What you are telling me is that this youngster Carlos Johnson deserves for someone to give him a break also; and that you are willing to be the some-one to take that chance." "Yes Judge Evans, I guess I am saying that." He sat back in his chair. "I hope you are sure, because I am going to give you that opportunity and him that break we've talked about. He will appear in my court room Monday and if you are there and the probation department doesn't object I will put him in your custody on a temporary trial basis, OK." Beaming, "Yes Your-Honor!"

Two years before these event Danny and Doris had gotten married after he came back home from the Olympics. They were a young happy couple who were looking forward to a life together; the only dark cloud was the death of her grandmother Ms. Edna. She had died that same year and left Doris the one-hundred acre farm that had to be worked to be profitable. Billy had gone on to become an ordained minister and became pastor of a congregation at a church in another state. Danny had hoped that he and his new bride could settle down in a big city where he could go on to obtain his Master's Degree in Education. Doris was set on doing everything she could to not lose the farm that had been in their family sense the end of the civil-war. There had been some heated exchanges until Billy came up with a suggestion. "Danny you always talked about having a home for disadvantages kids, and your wife has this big old farm here that has to be tended right." Both looked at him question mark on their face. "It's simple turn the farm into a home or community that the kids can live on fix up and work the land; that way you both can get what you want." Giving that wide grin upon having successfully solved a dilemma. They both looked at each other and smiled "Now why didn't we think of that." Danny interjected. "I think it will work on one condition Billy that is if we deal with their physical needs you will have to help us with their spiritual well-being, Ok." They all smiled in agreement hugging to seal the deal.

The juvenile court system is undermanned and over-crowded, with an assembly line like atmosphere of young people being brought in front of the magistrate to receive whatever punishment as the court dimmed appropriate. Judge Evans was a man of his word as he explained to the teen standing before him the reason and conditions for rendering his decision. "Because of the fact that someone has stepped forward in your behalf, and is willing to put themselves along with the reputation of their organization to take a chance with helping you I'll do the same. I am going to place you in the custody of Mr. Daniel Brown and his organization known as Y.P.H. (Young Peoples Home Community) as a probationer period of two years providing that you remain in his custody without incident, malice, nor commission of a crime or flight which in your case would be considered an escape and flight from the law, which is an adult federal felony crime punishable by serving the rest of the probation in a federal prison." The Judge was dead serious as he explained. "You getting a brake here son by the court and people who don't know you but are willing to take a chance on you because they believe you deserve it. This is a great opportunity for you to turn your life in the right direction; I hope you appreciate this and don't let yourself or these people down, is that clear. The young man stood there with an air of defiance, yet fragile like a small animal caught in a trap in which he needed help getting out of. "Yes Your Honor, that's clear." Puzzled expression written on his face.

Danny introduced himself as they headed out the court house to an awaiting vehicle that would take them to their final destination. He tried small talk as the boy looked him up and down. "What you say your name is dude?" "Well it isn't that, just call me Danny." "Look man I don't know you, what you want from me?" Danny pulled into a gas station. "I realize you don't know me or where we are going or how this all came about so it's like this. I made someone a promise, who isn't with us anymore that I would do all I could to help you receive a chance in life." The teen seemed baffled. "What you mean man? And who you talking about?" Danny had been dancing around the answer, so now it was time to come out with it. "I talked to your dad not long ago and his request was for" The boy interrupted seething with bitterness. "I ant got no dam dad, so you wasting your time." "You right about one thing you don't have a dad he is dead, he was put to death in a Federal Prison last week, but his finally request was to help keep you from ending up in prison, so time will tell if this is a waste of my time."

For the first time Carlos was able to let the wall down and show some feeling. However still unsure of what those feelings might be, then he blurted out. "Why he leave me, why I have to be alone?" Tears had welled in the young man eyes, as he turned his head not wanting Danny to see a child's pain. Danny started the engine as he pulled out of the parking lot heading for the highway. "I know what you are going through, I never even got a chance to meet my father he was killed in the Viet Nam War, and my mother is terminal with cancer as we speak." I found people that I could trust and count on for support in my time of need none of us has to go it alone, because we can't do it alone. I hope you will grow to like our community because we treat everyone like family at Y.P.H." The wall went back up as the teen looked somewhat detached not yet ready to buy into the idea. "Yea man, what-ever you say I'll hang for a while to see what's up."

For most of the rest of the journey they rode in silence, on the highway that was taking them through Ohio. Danny would stop for gas and ask the young man if he wanted something to eat or stop at a rest stop on their long journey. He realized that the teen had lived a hard and lonely life where the trust in another human being was one of the last things on his list. They were in Dayton Ohio near the I-75 interchange as he handed the young man a large bill telling him go and pay for the gas while he checked the oil and other fluids in the Mini-Van. As the young man was walking into the station he looked at the money then glanced back at Danny with puzzled expression on his face. Danny was so busily checking up under the hood that he didn't even look up to see where the boy was.

He paid for the gas came back to the Van handing Danny the change. As he looked across the street at the bus just pulling off from its stop. "How did you know I wouldn't take the money and run leaving you hear with your head up under the hood wondering how could I have let that happen because, I done been played?" "I didn't" as he finished pumping the gas, then getting in the Van to resume their journey. The boy countered. "You wasn't even paying me no attention dude, I could have disappeared with your money and you would not have seen me anymore." He said complete perplexed. "I know, but trust has to start at some-time somewhere, besides how far and how long would you run before you were caught, and then what?" "But you don't know me man, so why should you care what happens to me?

I don't care about what happens to you." Danny appeared to stare into the great beyond as they cruised down the highway. "Dr. King once said if we don't learn how to live as brothers, we'll parish as fools. Your father and mine were like brothers who had concern for each-others well-being. I think we owe it to ourselves and them to try and do the same." Carlos the troubled youth who didn't believe anyone cared looked Danny up and down. The hard look in his eyes began to soften as the snarl began to turn into a smile. It was plain to see that a change in this boys thinking and behavior was going to help him grow into a more well-rounded along with a kinder and gentler young man.

As they came over the hill into a valley Danny pointed to a group of buildings nestled in the middle of a picturesque lush farmland. "There it is our own Shangri-La, and it can be yours too. There is no such thing as an escaped person or one who tries to run away. If you notice there are no walls, barbed wire fences, or locked gates." He drove up to one of the buildings stopped and looked directly into Carlos eyes. "Regardless of what you think about your father, mother and anyone else in this world, somebody up there is giving you another chance at life and it's your responsibly to get things right in your life. The young man climbed out of the vehicle following Danny into one of the buildings that took on the appearance of a small bungalow. The boy was on the verge of a new life that if he stayed and gave himself a chance could turn his life around.

Before going any further it is important to look back and see how all this came about and begin to put the pieces of this jig-saw puzzle together.

Every story has a beginning and in a lot of cases many persons story can begin even before they are born. For some of our characters this is profoundly true because it is the fathers who have to be recognized for being at the tip of the spear in the war in the jungles over there that put into play the introduction of events to come in the asphalt jungle over here. There is no doubt the 1960's saw more turmoil in America than any-time since the civil war and the ones who lived and were a part of those times had no idea of the effect it would have on them, their children, and their children's children. This story starts out as the love story between two young people whose hopes were just to share their lives together. It begins half way around the world in that place many Americans didn't even know existed but was to become a house hold word for most and a battle cry for that 'radical generation', and of course the ice bird that this great ship of America ran into almost sinking it and everything it stood for.

CHAPTER 2

PICTURE OF LOVE

The young man sat on a tree stump with the look of love written on his face and a smile on his lips. He took the picture out of his pocket one more time with his mind drifting back to that night it was taken. It was a night of all nights that he would remember for as long as he lived. He and his fiancé had gone to an intimate nightclub to celebrate with old friends for his going away party.

The Cage Lounge was in the heart of D. C.'s entertainment district, a popular spot where couples mingled in a cozy atmosphere and tonight they were playing the popular love ballads of today, mixed in with a blast from the past. The young lovers found a table in the corner and order drinks. She put her hand on his, looking longingly into his eyes. "When we going to get married darling?" Squeezing her hand gently he replied, "I love and want you to be with me Terri, but I think we should wait until I get back." Her eyes and heart dropped. With sincerity in his voice he added. "Baby, you know I love you, there will never be anyone else for me. I'll love you and no one else, until the day I die. But we should wait because we don't know what will happen." They sat quietly for a few moments just looking into one-another's eyes with love in their hearts.

The lights in the club were dimmed as the D. J put on the love jam by the one of their favorite groups, <u>Stairway to Heaven</u> by the O.J.'s he asked, "Beautiful lady, May I have this dance?" She blushed, her dimpled smile. "Of course," she answered. He took his woman in his arms holding and squeezing her tight as they danced across the floor. Two lovers were suspended in another world while the mellow song of the O.J.s filled the room. The music stopped, he kissed her tenderly and they sat down. Moments later a shapely woman walked over to their table, bringing them out of their trance. "Terri, is that really you?" With the look of surprise, "Ilene!" Terri jumped up and both women began hugging and giggling likes two hysterical young teens. "It's been ages since I've seen you girl." They were high school chums and hadn't seen one-another since graduation. Ilene was the school's homecoming queen and Terri was voted 'most adorable.' "I heard you were moving to Baltimore." "Yea girl, my man just got home and we're gonna get married before he goes back." Ilene exclaimed, bubbling with joy, "Oh Ilene, this is my fiancé, Brent." He stood to shake her hand. "What would you like me to order for you?" He asked pulling up an empty chair. She glanced over her shoulder eyes searching the room. "My honey went to use the phone." Upon catching sight of him she waved for the man to come over to the table.

He looked quite striking in his dress green army uniform with neatly pressed pants tucked inside spit-shined boots. The soldier was an Air Borne Ranger, a member of the 101's unit of paratroopers called the 'Screaming Eagles' which were the elite warriors that had distinguished themselves from the battle of the Bulge in the second World War, to Korea and now in the central highlands of Vietnam. On the breast of his uniform were several medals with a combat emblem and airborne insignia. The man seemed to stand at attention as Ilene introduced him. "This is E-5 Sargent Mat Williams, my war hero." Brent was feeling hospitable. "Sit down; the first round is on me and my baby." As the soldier sat Brent couldn't help but admire how good the muscular man looked in his uniform. "Hey man, you been to the Nam?" The war and where it was fought in the jungles over there in the Southeast Asian nation that the U.S.'s had committed half-million troops, who were stuck in a quagmire was given that dubious name. "Yeah, just got back to the world." Which was any place in the U.S that soldiers came back to, "Ilene told me you are going into the service soon yourself?" Brent looked solemn, "I was drafted and will go to be sworn in, then leave for basic training Monday morning. "That's why I came to wish you good luck; the war is still raging like wildfire." Pointing to his leg, "I was hit and received a Purple Heart over there."

Matt leaned back in his chair. "I will never forget the first day I arrived. When we got off the plane the heat hit us like a wall of hot steam. Choppers were landing and taking off while GI's were running all over the place. An officer read our names off and led us through the confusion. The next thing I remember is that horrible smell as we walked past these rows of black bags on the ground one guy asked 'Is that what I think it is?" The officer smirked, "Yeah that will be most of you in a couple of weeks. The guy puked. He wasn't lying. They sent us up to Da Nang; GI's called it the 'killing zone' because most people who left there came back in one of those black bags. I was hit during the Tet Offensive when the North Viet Nam regulars came like locus over the DMZ and overran our firebase. Charlie's so good with them mortars he can drop one in a basket from five hundred yards. This war that we done got ourselves in don't make no sense, we losing too many good men and for what, we can't stop them people from getting there country back." Shaking his head, "It just doesn't make any sense."

For a while longer they enjoyed each other's company, and then it was time for the friends to part. Terri and Ilene said their good-byes. Brent held out his hand, but instead of shaking it Matt embraced him. "God be with you, Bro." Brent just stood for a moment after the couple exited the club. A woman with a camera in her hand walked up to him. "Would you and your lady like having your picture taken?" He looked at Terri. "Of course." They took a seat in a booth set aside for them. Terri snuggled up close to her man. "Darling, this will be our last picture together before I go in." She put her head on his shoulder. "Don't say last baby, cause better not nothing happen to my tall handsome sugar man." The camera clicked.

At that moment the young man snapped back to reality, looking around. Here is where he really was deep in the steaming hot jungle, smack in the middle of what was described to him once as the 'killing zone', with guys who were scared as he was. Well, Corporal Brent Brown knew one thing; in twenty-nine days and a wake up (thirty days left before his tour of duty in Viet Nam is up) he would be going back home and getting married to his sweet heart. He was about to put the picture back in his flak jacket pocket. "INCOMING!" (A word GI's used to warn each other about a mortar or rocket attack). All hell broke loose as the platoon's whole world erupted in a series of violent explosions. Earth, metal, and flesh were flung through the air as fireballs landed everywhere. Thick black smoke and the smell of gunpowder and burning flesh lingered in the air, the attack was over almost soon as it started. Wounded soldiers were crying and screaming for help. Others walked in a daze of disbelief, looking at the mangled bodies strewn over the landscape.

In their world death could come like rain out of the sky at any second it was taboo to get close to another soldier because tomorrow he might be dead and they didn't have time for grieving. The search and destruction of the enemy took all thoughts and energy. Personal feelings could defocus GI's causing them to drop their guard for a moment and possibly lose their lives. "How many casualties, Sargent?" taking his helmet off looking around. "Four dead and six wounded, Sir," they hit us pretty hard." Lieutenant Patrick Edwards picked up a picture from the ground. "Sargent comes over here for a moment." Sargent James Ryan walked over to the platoon leader. "Looks like one of the men and his wife or girlfriend." The Sargent dropped his head, "Yes sir, and seems that is all that is left of Corporal Brent Brown, it seems Charlie used the stump he was sitting on to zero in on our position." The lieutenant shook his head. "Oh my God, they dropped one of those mortar rounds right in his lap. He never knew what hit him. Did you know him well, Sargent?" Lying, to hold back the tears, "A little bit sir." Sargent Ryan knew who the girl on the picture was well as the dead soldier. How many times had he and the Corporal laid on their bunks, all the way back to A.I.T. (Advanced Infantry Training before coming to Viet Nam), talking about that picture, home, their girls and their families. He even remembered when Brent invited him home upon their leave before coming over seas, after he got a letter about the death of his father, in which Brent was going with him to help him bury his father. He could still picture Mama Brown feeding and fussing over him like he was a family member. He thought about lovely Terri, who introduced him to her sister giving his life meaning again. James Ryan knew how devastated and broken hearted both women would be upon hearing about Brent's death. He also reflected on what Corporal Brown's death would mean to him, too. He loved the ever smiling, young man like the brother he never had.

A few minutes ago they were taking a break in this endless jungle and now blood, bodies and death were everywhere. The radio operator frantically called for help reporting their position. "Red leader come in. We need air support, under heavy fire, come in Red leader!" Seconds' later jets appeared over—head, spreading napalm just outside their parameter. The 2nd platoon had suffered the heaviest causalities as the Sargent inspected the condition of his men and equipment then scrambled toward the radio operator. "Did you call chopper's medevac for the wounded along with the air support for us?" "Yes Sargent", the look of horror in his eyes. The Sargent then walked over to the platoon leader. "Here are the rest of the dead men's dog tags and personal effects Sir." Just then the roar of the hewies blades could be heard landed the birds in the cleared out thicket.

After the dead and wounded were loaded onto choppers Sargent Ryan, Lieutenant Edwards, and the rest of the platoon climbed aboard theirs. As they lifted up over the jungle, Sargent Ryan looked down at the clearing and the tears began to flow. He thought about losing so many men so fast in the middle of nowhere and of course his good friend. A verse he had read while in school from some book came to mind. 'Life must go on though good men die. Life must go on we know not why.' So many died so young, so far away from home.

This wasn't the last time Sargent Ryan was going to be among young men dying so far away from home. He signed up for another tour of duty and after coming home on leave to visit his father's grave, was assigned to another battalion that was on their way to Southeast Asia. His unit was the 501'st Infantry who had all trained together and came to Viet Nam together from Gray Air Field outside of Fort Hood and about ten miles from the military town of Killen Texas. He remembered the day before his battalion along with the 506th and 240th infantry battalions were to be despoiled with all their equipment and personal (bag &baggage, lock loaded) into the C 1-30 and C 1-40 transport planes heading across the big pond.

Just before leaving they had all been confined to the post

to discourage AWOL all leaves and passes were canceled and after duty hours most of the men went either to the chapel or back to their companies. Of course their barracks were at the air field away from the main post, so the men pack cloths, equipment and cleaned their weapons. Along with some drinking as they wrote letters home, watch movies, or listened to music in their own quarters. Each of the apartments like units housed a company that was broken down into platoon that had four squads on each floor. Sargent Ryan was platoon leader for the 2nd platoon he and most of the men in his platoon were packed into one room. Moral was high as they played, cards, were telling jokes, and even dancing with one-another; generally doing all they could to booster one-another's spirits.

The Sargent barked out orders to his men. "I want all of you to have your over-seas shot cards. Make sure all the field gear and jungle wear is packed into your duffle bags I mean everything from mess gear to gas mask, socks, fatigues, tooth brush, shaving kit, and jungle boots. Make double sure that all weapons, M-16's, 50 calibers, 30 calibers, your 45's and even those bayonets and any other weaponry, are cleaned and polished. This isn't going to be no picnic in the park that we going to its a real war going on in them dam jungles and the difference between life and death will depend on whether or not your equipment works or not meaning under all the extreme conditions. The first Sargent will be through the barracks to check to make sure his company 'Bravo' wills past the field I inspection. No sooner the words left his lips "Top" the company First Sargent walked through the door. He was dressed in battle gear which included helmet, a flak jacket, jungle fatigues with a 45. Colt pistol strapped to his side. "Attention." Sargent Ryan ordered. Everyone scrambled to their bunks wall lockers opened, foot lockers opened, and bunks made up tight enough to bounce a quarter off, with personal toiletries and personal items laid out for Top to see. And he went over them with the eye of a real military man who had made this his life's work.

In fact he had come from the Hills of Tennessee in a place they called the Valley of the three forks It was a place of where poor Appalachian farmers who took pride in being in the same Valley that Sargent Alvin York, the most decorated American war hero of WWI. First Sargent Ridgeway had been a young lad of barley 17 when he convinced his parents to sign for him to join the Army just before the Japanese surrendered in September of 1945. He was disappointed at not being able to fight in the war, but his turn came when North Korea came across the 38th Parr ell that was separating them from South Korea. He was one of the lucky ones that survived the battle for 'Pork Chop' hill. Now here he was again dressed in battle gear ready to take on another enemy in another war of South against the North.

He walked from one soldier to the next going over them,

and their bunk along with their equipment with the eye of a master who could spot anything out of place, missing or with the slightest smudge. Sargent Ryan walked a step behind him ready to put down any infraction. "This rifle is fealty son, what in the hell do you expect to hit with this dirty thing, it will blow up in your face." He stepped briskly to another bunk as he snatched everything off it onto the floor. He stepped to another soldier's bunk and as he examined everything on it he called out. "Son, where yo dam shaving kit." The young soldier with a shaky voice blurted out. "I have never used a razor sir." Top seemed irritated. "First thing I ant no officer, I work for my living, second thing as he looked around the room at all the fresh faces many with not a trace of hair on their faces. You all. Your job is staying alive. "You'll might not shave now but when we get over there you gonna act like and look like harry apes in the jungles. "Gentleman this ant no resort, and you'all not going on no dam vacation. This the real deal, never forget, that is your job, because if you do one of them gooks gonna have your ears, nose, eyes and teeth or any other part he wants on his charm necklace for a souvenir. It was so quite you could hear a pin drop. I mean I want this place and you equipment ready for a full field inspection at 0800 hours when the Corneal comes through. Turning to Sargent Ryan, "Take over and made sure every swinging ass is ready by morning." "Men revelry is at 0600 hr. break-fast at 0700 hr. A full field inspection at 0800 hr, Then we march out to the field bag and baggage lock and load out to our air field where those huge C 1-40's for the men and the C 1-30's for all our things will take us on our little ride." One of the men nervously asked. "We gonna make any stops Sarge?" "This ant no dam taxi service but we make a stops in California. We will then fly to the Hawaiian Islands to refuel before that big hop across the pound." Each man in his own way was doing what he could to muster the courage to face their greatest fear the unknown.

Now here they were in what seemed like quicker than a flash facing the unknown and the enemy in a battle to cut off North Vietnamese's reinforcements from Laos by attacking Hill 937. Along with the 506th infantry battalion and the 101st airborne troops moving up the highly sloped hill about 2 miles from the Laotian border. Their opposition besides the rugged terrain and a mountain towering some 937 meters or over 3,000 feet high was the North Viet Nam 29th regiment that were part of the 1968 Tet Offensive, called the 'Pride of Ho Chi Minh'. The U.S. troops were also aided by 2 South Vietnam battalions known as ARVN units who were to help a Marine unit cut off the highway they were using for reinforcement. The battle ragged from May 10 until May 20 of 1969 along narrow trails snaking through the dense foliage with enemy hiding in bunkers that couldn't be seen from the air. The dense jungle was eventually stripped away by indirect fire from Jets spreading Napalm, with some 'agent orange'. However it wasn't until the dogged squad and platoon-level action that the enemy was finally subdued, after countless tracks up that mud die bloody hill that our troops won the day. The pace and price was thoroughly unanticipated by American forces. Hill 937 was dubbed as "Hamburger Hill" by the American soldiers who fought there, it was suggested that those who fought on the hill were "chewed up like a hamburger" and was compared to the Battle of Pork Chop Hill fought during the Korean War.

Sargent Ryan survived with only minor shrapnel wounds. He left Viet Nam with pictures of many of the guys he had served with who had died before the people of their country knew they had lived. But he would never forget them their images and faces were branded into his brain. Now that their battle was over he could admit that he loved all of them, because they were his band of brothers. He knew he had to get in touch with Terri and make sure she receive Brent's picture along with other personal items. It might even be necessary for him to fly all the way to Boston where she had moved to make sure she received the things personally. He had no idea what was in store for him as he was coming back to the good old U.S. of A.

The nation's mood toward the Viet Nam war had completely changed. When he stepped off an airplane, uniform pressed boots shinned he was greeted with boos and name calling, someone even tried to spit on him. He was being looked at as the enemy not those persons that had taken so many of his friends lives in those jungles. To him it was baffling and confusing situation, because while fighting in those jungles all he could think about was getting back to what was called the world (the U.S.A.) or home, yet when he got back he was treated like a stranger in his own hometown. Things were so weird and different until his mind began to drift back to the 'killing zone' where his true loyal friends who made him feel like a brother were at.

After drifting around awhile he finally found his way to Boston where he was determined to make sure Terri received her husband, Corporal Brown's personal items. He began to wrestle with the idea of going back in the service even if it meant being sent back on another tour of Viet Nam, anything would be better that wandering around like the man with no country or home to call his own. His hometown was a small place right outside of Atlanta Georgia named Royston that was mostly and Island surrounded by water, that he wasn't eager to return there. As he boarded the plane for Boston's Logan Airport he thought about that time he and the remainder of his Platoon climbed onto the choppers in the middle of the jungle on their way back from Da Nang, it seemed like an eternity ago.

He found himself at the door of a unit in the Roxbury

section of Boston that Corporal Brown had given him. As he was about to ring the bell the door flung open, he was shocked to see Terri standing there tears in her eyes and a small child clinging to her leg. "Oh my god for a moment all I could think of was Brent coming down the street." She reached out Sargent Ryan embraced her. "I know he dead but just for a moment my mind told me he had come back to us." Reaching down picking up the child. "This his son, whom he never met." Sargent Ryan smiled as he greeted the boy, "Hey there little man what's your name and how old are you?" The boy smiled back. "I Danny and me two." "It's almost like seeing Brent all over again", turning to Terri. "Yes and I thank god for the gift."

She invited him in as they went and sat down. "I am so glad you called and told me you were coming, you don't know how much this means to me just seeing his best friend again, it brings back those happy memories of when he brought you home with him that time and we all celebrated together just before you two went to that awful place." She dropped her head letting out a couple more sobs. "So this your sister and her husband's place?" Looking around, as if hoping to catch a glimpse of her. "Yea they got married in Chicago before moving here with their son, they just left to pick him up from one of his school friends house, me and my son moved here from D.C. after Brent's death." Looking at him curiously, "How come you didn't come back and ask for Shelia s hand? I think she was waiting and hoping that you would ask." Shaking his head, "I don't know those were some confusing times I guess I thought I was unworthy, with so much racial tension in the air, or maybe I just wanted to die like so many of my friends. Anyway I came to bring you a few of his personal things first." As he handed her some pictures, a watch, medallion, and a medal she responded. "I am truly great full that you are doing this for me but what are you going to do for yourself?"

"When I got to the States it seems like I could see things for what they are, I mean the war over there and what is happening over here and it seems like the real war is being fought out here on the home front. The soldiers like me that fought over in the Nam are being seen by many as the enemy because we have been fighting on the wrong side. For a while I was mixed up and confused, thinking I owed it to all my boys who didn't come back, to go back and risk my life again, but now I know the real fight is here. With the riots and unrest, so many of our major cities in flames, college campuses being seized, and of course great leaders being murdered right before our eyes makes me feel that there is some sinister force that has been unleashed to take the power away from the people.

There is a big rally that is going to be held in your home town of D.C. that I want to be a part of. There will be thousands of war veterans, college students, religious leaders, and just plan everyday Americans who want to stage a protest and get some answers about what is really going on in this country and even some going before Congress to find answers about how we got involved in an unwinnable war, and when we going to get out, it ant about saving face it's about saving those young lives far as we concerned. This war don't make any sense at all I can see that very clearly now that I'm out of the jungles and not having to see death, or worry about when my number will come up. We were fighting an enemy that you couldn't identify, he may be No.1 boy in the day time and a Viet Kung fighter at night. It was a dirty war that gave me a feeling of guilt and shame when one of my buddies got killed and we had to kill half a village to seek revenge or find answers."

Ryan shook his head. "Believe you me the Viet Kung and their people were not the only ones getting shot by M-16's or blown up with American grenades. That's what made this war so crazy. A lot of Officers and Non-Coms had to sleep with one eye open and one had on their weapon in our own compounds. It was some guys that were so gee ked up off that Heroin or Opium, and I mean the shit was pure, that they became killing machines who were in their own crazy mixed up and insane world. These guys wouldn't allow anyone to say anything to them or give them any order that they opposed. In one of the units I was attached to before going to Hamburger Hill the First Sargent was shot in the back with an M-16 round while the C.O and one of his company officers were 'fragged' by a grenade (blown up) in another. Any—time soldiers turn against superior commanders in a war zone and start taking their lives something is awfully wrong with the reason why they are fighting and dying and the fear of not thinking there is no hope for a way out."

As he walked to the door, "Anyway, say goodbye to your sister and tell her I wish here all the happiness. I am on my way to Washington D.C. Mall where many of us Viet Nam Veterans from all branches of the service will be protesting, hell even some of the guys will go before the Senate to testify. I met this one guy who was an Officer on one of those P.T boats in the Mekong Delta that said it will defiantly be called to testify." Sargent Ryan waved to Terri and her son as he disappeared heading toward the setting sun.

He found himself boarding a Greyhound Bus heading towards Washington D.C. And while riding in deep thought about a conversation he had with one of the other G.I's he met while waiting in a terminal on one of his many flights home. He had struck up a conversation with a Corporal Jackson who had been in the same Regiment he was at Fort Hood Texas. "Yea Sarge our Battalion was out there training in the woods and mountains near Gray Air Base like yours." Talking as if trying to jog Ryan's memory. "I was in the

I.G.

240th Infantry Battalion and you were Platoon Sargent over at the 501st unit of Paratroopers." the light bulb came on. "Oh Yea!" he exclaimed. "There were four Battalions of us training together; ah the other two were the 35th Infantry and the 506th Paratroopers. We all were due to ship out for Viet Nam after training, the only ones that I can recall going over to the Nam was my 501st and the 506th, and so what happened to you two." Ryan said sarcastically.

The Corporal gave him a no non sense look. "The Paratrooper Units went first so you'll were deployed in March of 1968, is that not right?" Ryan agreed. "Yes but of course." "On April 4th of 1968 Dr. King was assonated at that Motel in Memphis, and riots broke out in cities all across the United States. Two of the major ones were in Washington D.C. and Chicago, both were ragging with fire, looting, and killing. The one in Washington was four block from the White House burnings and gun-fire in the streets. The Capital of the United States was latterly under seized and the Government was gripped with fear that it would spread to where the President lived or where Congress resided. The Powers that be considered themselves in a War and had no alternatives but to send for Federal Troops. So the 35th Infantry Battalion was deployed to D.C. in—stead of De Nang Viet Nam." Sargent Ryan sat back somewhat dismayed. "Wow" The Corporal continued. "And while that was going on the same thing was happening in

Chicago, Mayor Daily's town and one of the strong holds of the Democratic Party that was incidentally hosting the Democratic Convention in the summer of 1968. My unit, had been held back at Fort Hood as if someone knew a battle, and I say war not riot because that's what it was, someone felt it was the event that was planned for. Dr. King was killed on "Good Friday" and by Monday morning we were being loaded bag and baggage, lock and load on those huge C 1-30 transports planes heading for War Zone Chicago Ill. To the Sargent it was like a blow that hit him in his gut. How could the same Military that was fighting for the rights and freedom of a People somewhere else do battle with its own people over their rights and freedom. "Yea Sarge what kind of dam crazy shit is that, Uncle Sam was a war on two fronts, half of the Regiment was sent to fight in Viet Nam, while the other half was sent to fight in the 'Battle of the Cities.' I am from Detroit (Motown) but you know what was so dam scary some people like me had relatives on the South side of Chicago, so what kind of deadly game was that?"

Sargent Ryan sat quietly the rest of the trip taking it all in and what it all meant. It was as if he and many like him hadn't lived their own lives it was almost like some giant puppet master had been pulling the strings with them being on the other end of the life and death struggle in which they had no control or say over. Just to think when he was a boy on that farm in Georgia, he would go into town with his father who was the over-seer for the Cambridge family plantation that raised cotton and soy beans crops. He had taken it for granted that he and his father could walk in the front door of the diner while the other black plantation workers had to wait outside or if they were lucky to go in the back door and get some of the left overs. The straw boss directly under his father would go over to the general store or supply place to pick out the things that were needed for the farm, while he and his father sat at the counter drinking on ice cold sodas water with the other patrons. Sometimes they would sit for a couple hours as his father was chewing the fat with his buddies from childhood as the two "boys" that were with them had to try and find shade or just sit on the curb waiting.

That's the way things were back in those days, white folks could go into places eat, shop, sit down and in-joy a cold drink on a hot day when and where they wanted. The blacks, even the ones that they knew and had worked with for years, not only were not allowed but were litterly reduced to the status of a loyal pet that had to wait on them in more ways than one until they had finisher having their fill. White's like them didn't see it as odd or wrong and that they were taking a disadvantage of the 'Niggras', that just how the order of things went and had gone on for generations. There was no doubt that the white race was superior everyone knew that even if you was what they called 'poor white trash' you was better than any 'Niggras'. They never even thought about how blacks felt about things like that, whites were doing them a favor by letting them be with them.

He and his father lived in the small house between the main one and the barn while the other hands lived in those shot gun shacks scattered in the back where they share-cropped the land. His Mother had died of Typhoid when he was ten years old, and sense then his friends grandmother, Miss. Mozilla would cook, clean, chop wood, bathe him, and put him in bed while taking care of both houses. Amos his friend was her oldest grandson, but both boys were the same age and she always treated them the same. He would fill badly the mornings they went to school after the two had eaten the grits and fat back she gave them for breakfast. The yellow school bus would come to pick him and other white kids up for school that was less than a mile down the road while Amos and the other black kids, had to walk five miles down that dusty or sometimes Rainey mud filled road. No one back then ever questioned it that was just how things were. After school, He and Amos would go back to doing things the way they had done all along. They were still friend even though they weren't equal.

His father was indifferent toward blacks and always told him that when he grow—up he would have to treat them like he was their master. He and Amos dad had been friends when they were kids but now he had to make sure that as men each of them knew their place, so they didn't socialize or chew the fat anymore. However the thing that really upset him was when Miss Mozilla went to what his father called that 'rabble rouser' preachers speech even though his father told her if she did Mr. Chambers might kick her off his land. She was one of those strong independent minded black women who wouldn't allow anybody to tell her who to be around. She had gone up to Atlanta with other members of her church to listen to the young Martin Luther King talking about organizing a march on Washington, and when she got back Mr. Chambers told her to get off his land or he would have her arrested.

His father was furious and started screaming at her, after all they depended on her for everything. He got in her face called her a no good black 'bitch' she shot back with 'red neck peckerwood'. He then balled his fist up and knocked her down, for back talking a white man, something that just wasn't done back then. He was hurt beyond belief as Amos broke out in tears as lifting her off the floor. The boy held onto one of her arms, his father screamed at him "Let that Nigger Bitch stay on the floor." He couldn't believe his father could be that cruel to someone who had done so much for them. She had to leave the county, to go and live with her other son or face the Klu Klux Klan's punishment for daring to defy her white overseer. Amos and his father were devastated, filled with fear and uncertainty, because the boy's father and some of the other whites looked at them with suspicion. It was right then and there that his whole perception of things changed. White kids like himself were exposed to what was being said about civil rights for black folks and the whole issue about race, decimation, segregation, and equality for all. It took that to let him see that the way he had been raised was wrong, at least when it came to people. All he could see was that Miss Mozzal, Amos and his father always treated him like he was part of their family.

After that the close relationship he had with his dad grew more distant with time. The father started drinking heavily and they got further and further apart until when he was seventeen he signed to let his son join the Army so that they wouldn't become bitter enemies, it was then that as he grew through the ranks of service that his understanding and acceptance for others not by color but from the content of their character grew into the leader of men that he would become. He looked out the window of the bus as it rolled down the highway saying to him that there is nothing permanent but change and that everyone and everything in life must change and adapt or parish. Just before going to Viet Nam he had to bury his father thinking that his only wish had been for his father to see it that way before he died.

I.G.

James Ryan was just glad that joining the Army gave him a chance to see and meet people of all colors, backgrounds, ethnic groups, and religions. He was part of a team of guys and girls who had enough trust in each other that they would sacrifice; even putting their lives on the line to make sure that no one was left behind. As the war in Southeast Asia intensified he understood that the man in the fox hole next to him might be a 'brother from Detroit' or a 'Farm boy from Iowa, it didn't matter where he was from only that he would put his trust in and depend on the fact that they could be in a fire fight back to back until the last of their ammunition was used up. He got that chance when he was waiting to be deployed to Viet Nam. The same year that the draft had put a record number of young Americans from all parts of the country, from all backgrounds, all colors, and all walks of life, into that olive green uniform being called G.I. issued.

It was during his Jungle training at Fort Polk Louisiana's 'Tiger Land' that he met Brent Brown the recruit fresh out of Basic Training that he was able to bind a friendship like he had done as a boy back on that farm in Georgia. They bunked together, ate together, trained together and shared stories of family and the way their lives had once been before they became the guest of Uncle Sam. Although one had grown up in the country and the other in the city along with the obvious of one black and the other white, they felt a closeness that transcends all boundaries of color, background, upbringing or social presser. Just before they were to leave the States for combat duty Ryan received the news of his father's death, so it was Brent who accompanied his friend home to bury his dad. After the funeral he convinced Ryan to spend the rest of his leave as his guest with his family in D. C. The two soldiers had an unforgettable time as the love of Brent's life Terri introduced him to her sister who became very fund of the 'Georgia Boy' with the four of them spending most of their time together. It wasn't until the last week of their leave that James Ryan left them to visit his father's only remaining sister who had taken ill herself. The next time the two were together was on the battle field in the Central Highlands of Viet Nam.

All the horror of the war and losing his friends was behind him as he surmised he must do this in order to deal with the painful past. Now he was on his way to doing something he never even thought possible for him to do when he first put on the U.S Army uniform. He was not alone there were many other veterans, college students, clergy man, housewives, mothers, fathers, and just plain everyday Americans from all walks of life, all back grounds, and colors getting off buses. By the time they arrived at the Washington Mall their numbers had swelled to the thousands. The crowd occupied the entire mall between the Lincoln Memorial, where Dr. King gave his 'I Have a Dream' speech leading to the Washington Monument, even up to the gates of the White House and the President's residence. There seemed to be as many Military persons and Veterans as there were civilians all marching through the Mall down Pennsavanian Avenue carrying protest sign declaring peace, love, and the end to the Viet Nam War.

The Protesters moved through the streets well into the night carrying candles, stopping to light bond fires where many burned draft cards, and Government ID. The police presence was all around, on foot, horse—back, motor cycles, even having armed troops on roof tops. At first they merely observed with tense caution, but as the crowds grew on the following day many of the decorated Viet Nam veterans began taking their medals, citations and awards off tossing them into the reflecting pool. It seemed like then it was all that the authorities could take as they shot off tear gas canisters and with shields and batons began wading into the crowd, pushing, shoving and leading many off to jail. They felt that the desecration of Government property was the ultimate disgrace.

James Ryan although one of the protesters felt that he could do more if his voice was heard in another arena, as he arranged to put himself in position to go before a Congressional Committee. As it turned out although he was on the docket to give testimony in front of the Congressional Committee he ended up listening in the glary to the words of others who were called on to give their side of the issue. One of the witnesses was giving some compelling testimony about how the war had really taken a turn against the U.S since the Tet Offensive, giving rise to America pulling out all Military Forces. Some of the Congressman seemed stunned by the Lt's accounts of how so many of the soldiers of all ranks, and in all branches of the service really felt about fighting in a hopeless war. Places like the fire base at Ka San were brought up, the high price that was paid to take Hamburger Hill, and of course all the PO's and M.I.A's, as a result of the failed bombing missions over North Viet Nam. It was some riveting mind blowing accounting that the young officer laid bare before the Committee summing up how American Soldiers, whose average age was nineteen, had been put in the meat grinder and literally used for cannon fodder in the Jungles of Viet Nam.

After all the witnesses had been called and the testimony had been given it seemed like the winds of change of not only those who had protested the war all along, college students, militants, civil rights advocates, clergyman, and the families of those who had seen their love ones give the full measure, but now those who along with the President had committed men and arms. It seemed like this protest march having so many who had been over-there and had come back here with a different attitude were now having an effect to reverse the norm of thinking and those in position of power's perception of what America's role in Southeast Asia really should be. As Sargent Ryan stood before the Viet Nam War Memorial; the warrior who did his duty on the battle field looking out for his men came away with a sense of accomplishment. In his heart he knew that he had done his best to look out for and stand up for all those warriors who had given their lives for their Country.

CHAPTER 3

DANNY'S RUN

He could hear the clapping, cheering, and roar of the ecstatic crowd ringing in his ears as he rounded the track for a victory lap. Flash bulbs were going off in the stadium stands giving the appearance of thousands of lights. He thought about the people who were part of this great triumph. It was a long hard and sometimes hazardous journey this young man from the Roxbury projects of Boston had traveled. Now he was finally among the winners his long race was finished. How sweet the taste of victory is.

His mind went back to the day in-which his life had taken a 180 degree turn. He and his mother had gone to the Pizzeria to pick up their order, and just as they arrived a crowd was mumbling about some-body being shot attempting flight from a hold up. Danny pushed through the people and just as the medics were putting the youth's lifeless body into the ambulance, he froze with the look of horror on his face. His mother came up a moment later and screamed. "Thomas; oh god no!" Danny could still hear his mother's cries as the E.M.S drove away with his cousin's body. His and Thomas mothers were the last two sisters in their family left, and the two boys weren't just cousins but had grown up like brothers. Danny looked up to the older boy and wanted to be and live like him. Now his idol's life was gone snuffed out like a candle on a cold windy night.

At that time Thomas was about the only male in the family who the youth patterned him-self after. Danny never knew his father who died in the Viet Nam war. A picture of both his parents just before his father went off to war sat on the mantel and was one of his mother's prize possessions. His uncle Ike had a good heart, but like most of the adult males in their neighborhood, who was caught up in the grip. His whole life and thinking was centered in drugs, the getting, using, and finding ways and means to get more. Danny remembered the times he saw them all in that room shooting up, like zombies more dead than alive. He reasoned that a life of drug using or selling was not in his itinerary. His mother had made the decision some years earlier to move her and the boy closer to her only sister so the two of them who had lost the men in their lives could help and support each other. Many times in the Afro-American community the mothers are left to be both parents in their households. It has become an unfair burden placed on women's shoulders, to raise a family especially when male children are concerned.

One of those children was his cousin, whose street name was T. Man who had been leader of the most ruthless gangs in the projects. He and fellow gang members controlled the drug trade from Tremont to Mass. Ave. While Danny watched the E.M.S. pull away a cold chill came over him. It seemed like a voice whispered to him saying, if you take your cousin's path this to would be your fate. Right then the teen decided he must do whatever it took to stay away from that life. It wasn't easy either in Danny's world drugs and guns were easier to buy than candy, with gang members spreading them like a plague all over the community. The boys began to run, not out of fear but "out of sight outa of mind," his mother told him. "Some must run away to fight another day," His uncle advised him. So Danny ran every-where, to school, to the store, over his friend's house, and to the community center where he ran around their indoor track. And Danny stayed off the main streets, parks and spots where they exchanged their contraband. Danny remembered hearing the story about his great-great grandfather, a slave who had to run to his freedom from the red hills of Georgia, and with the aid of the underground railroad was able to make it all the way up to Detroit where a free black man helped him and others to escape to Canada on a boat he owned. Most of the long and arduous journey he was a step ahead of blood-hounds who were snapping at his heels. Now Danny was running for his freedom, from the gangs, violence, and drugs that were threatened to overtake his life. Many of the boys he was trying to keep away from had come from single parent homes as he had, being raised primarily by their mothers with the fathers either dead, in prison or just missing in action. Danny had made up in his mind that he wasn't going to be one of the casualties of this strange war that was being waged in the jungle of America's city streets and neighborhoods. Before that his mother had made the decision years earlier to move her and the boy closer to her only sister so the two of them who lost the men in their lives could help and support each other. Most of the women can be commended for doing a great job; it however has been too great a burden to place upon women, like the two sisters, shoulders to raise young men without the help of a man. After all there was the lure of the streets and the life style that offered quick fortunes with the price being paid of a fast life's reward of jails and death. His cousin who's street name was T. Man had been drawn like the moth to a flame.

By the time Danny entered high school he was like a diamond in the ruff, that receive polishing and training from the track and field coach that took a liking to the boy with the bright smile. Mr. Bronson saw raw talent in the boy so he guided, groomed, and taught him all the basics and techniques. It didn't take a whole lot because the tall well-built teen had grown into a real runner with long gazelle like strides. Danny made All—City and All-State becoming a celebrated runner in the 400 meters while anchoring the 4x400 relay team. The kid from the projects of Boston had become one of the best track and field runners in the nation winning a scholarship to one of the most prestigious collagen sport schools in the U.S. the one and only Tennessee State College. He would be the first one in his family to go to college. It had been not only for him but one of his mother's solemn dreams for her son to find a way out of the traps that many of the young men his age, including his cousin had fallen into, through education. He made a commitment to himself, well as his mother who had become a victim of breast cancer that he would be the best at whatever he strived to do no matter what it took. Now at Tennessee State he would have the opportunity to make good on his promise.

In the next two years Danny worked toward being a world class runner and accomplishing his dream of making the Olympic Team and represents his country. His relay team had already broken the College record and he was ranked as one of the top runners in the 400 meters in America. He and some fellow members of his team ran track in the spring and played football in the fall. His best friend on both teams, a kid by the name of Billy, who had grown up not too far from the campus were having the time of their lives as Fraternity brothers and big men on the campus. One day after they had finished practice, Billy the kid with the wide grin, who was lead off on the relay team, pulled up in his car. "Come go for a ride with me before you hit those books." The college campus was nestled right outside a small town with wide open country and several farm houses dotting the landscape. Billy drove down a lonely highway then turned onto a gravel road that seemed to lead nowhere. "Hey Billy, where are we going?" Danny turned to him with a concerned look on his face. "Out to Auntie Edna's she got a weak heart and I look in on her when I got time." After a few minutes he pointed to a house in the distance stopping just in front of it. Billy then jumped out the car ran up on the porch, opened the screen door and walked right in like he was the long lost son who had come home. After a few moments Danny climbed out of the car and followed.

In a way it could be considered like home to Billy who hadn't always been the easy going kid with the wide grin. He had grown up on a farm the son of a Mississippi share cropper who lived with his seven other brothers and sisters in one of those shot gun shacks, where his father barley eked out a living for them working from sun up to sun down on Mr. Charley's land in return for a portion to feed, house, and put cloths on his families back. Of course it never was enough being in constant debt to the landowner, which kept he and others like him crippled with poverty. Billy had to compete or wait for everything he received from the cloths on his back to the last crumb of food on the table. When he and his brothers were old enough they had to forgo school to help his father in the fields. The boy hated the thankless labor in the fields while he loved being in the class room where he felt free to read and dream. Back in the segregated South the education of black children took a back seat to them having to help bring the crops in. The boys especially, only went until the spring, which was planting time and seldom in the fall which was time to bring the harvest to market. The boy and his father were at odds with each other from the time he was thirteen until when he finally ran away.

He hopped freight and was heading north when he was forced to get off by the rail road detectives. It was a frightened, lonely and hungry boy that sat on a tie in the rail yard sobbing, that one of the train workers found late one night. The man took the boy home with him after hearing his story feeling the least he could do was to let his wife give him a hot meal. Mrs. Edna Mae Johnson took a liking to the lad from the beginning offering him a place to stay along with hot meals. It turns out she was a teacher at the newly integrated high school and she and her husband Mr. Leroy Johnson who was a train conductor on the railroad, were two of the most greatly admired and highly respected residents of the Tennessee town of well off black residents. He became as close to the couple as the son they never had. After getting in touch with his family Billy made the decision to stay with the Johnson's were he had the freedom to go to school and pursue his dream. Upon entering high school he too became a celebrated runner in helping to lead his small town track and field team to a state championship. The boy was good in all sports where he also won a scholarship to Tennessee State. The bitterness and despair turned into that wide smile as Billy found joy and happiness by obtaining victory in the world of sports.

"Auntie Edna it's me Billy your long lost boy done come home." A tiny wrinkled woman with snow white hair and twinkling eyes ran from the kitchen, hugging him like he was a long lost son. "I should whale your back side for waiting so long to come and see me" Billy shrugged his shoulders, "I just been busy with making the team and all gesturing to take focus off him "This here one of my best friends who on the team with me." As he nudged Danny toward the joyful woman, "Well you boys come on in the kitchen I'm baking some sweet potato pie and you can eat it while it's hot with a cold glass of lemonade. Everyone it the county knew Ms. Edna, she was always there with a kind word, smile, and good food for those in need and of course those award winning pies.

"Grandma, I just finished feeding the chickens, and."

The girl stopped in her tracks with startled look. "Oh excuse me I didn't know you had company grandma." Her bright bottom eyes met Danny's both motionless as they stared openly at each other She had long curly black hair fixed in a ponytail, with skin soft as a ripe Georgia Peach; his heart melted right there on the spot. Ms. Edna broke the spell, "Young man this granddaughter Doris, and she a freshman just starting at you'll college." Danny's heart was caught in his throat as he struggled to get the words out. "Glad to meet you." Extending her hand "Hello good to meet you." "And Billy how you been." Gently hugging him eyes still fastened on Danny. "Billy I see there truly is beauty down here on the farm." They all laughed. Ms. Edna turned to Billy. "Come out back wane show you our new born calf," whispering, "Give those two a chance to get acquainted."

Doris cut Danny another piece of pie brushing up against him. "Want some more lemonade?" "Yes thank you, the both of you ladies have a lovely farm." "Well thank you Danny Brown." He was somewhat taken aback that she knew his name, giving her a look of pleasant surprise. "I saw your picture and read about you in the campus newspaper, the story about you making a promise to your mother about obtaining a college education was inspiring." Her heart skipped a beat as she had secretly longed to meet him. Now fate had brought the two of them together. She sat next to him after pouring two glasses of lemonade. "I moved in with grandma after my mother died, he was a gentle soul who dedicated his life to his family and his job as a conductor on the railroad. He started out putting those big ties down then nailing the rails to them like the legendary John Henry, but he went on to being one of the first black conductors to work for the Chesapeake & Ohio railroad. He always stressed the importance of a college education. So I am going to major in Agronomy." With a serious look in her brightly smiling eyes. "That way I can get a degree and help grandma and others get the best use and most capacity out of their land. The American farmers feed over half the word, but are losing their farms at an alarming rate. We need to give those who have given so much to us all the support and knowledge we can for the good of this nation." Danny thought to himself, not only was she a beauty, but she also had a brain. At that moment two hearts and minds ran together and as Ms. Edna and Billy entered the kitchen love was in the air.

The rest of the summer the young couple was inseparable. One weekend at a picnic the two of them were sitting in the grass gazing out over the lake. It seemed like the fiery sun was slowly sinking into the water quenching a hot day. The rays made a shimmering pathway right up to their spot in the grass. She squeezed up against him as the two lovers held hands. "Doris I received a letter from home and my mother is sick, my Aunt who wrote me says that the entire test momma took, indicate she has breast cancer and it's very aggressively spreading to other parts of her body." Fear and doubt was written all over his face as he shook his head in agony. They embraced as the tears began to flow. "I am going home to Boston next week, and don't know when or if I will be back." Doris stiffened and pulled away. "No, you can't mean that, you can't leave school, not now." He held her tight and kissed her deeply. "Baby I love and will never leave you, after I go home and stay to make sure my mother alright then I am coming back for you darling." "I'm not talking about that, what I mean is that you can't leave school and your dream and a chance of a life time to compete in the Olympics, you once told me that was the most important thing to you." Danny started shaking his head with face buried in his hands. "Yes but my mother is terminal with cancer she needs me." Doris took a deep breath staring into what seemed to be the unknown. "I feel your pain and know what you are going through Danny." She was ringing her hands. "My mother died of Lupus and someone that was very close to her or should I say like a sister to her wanted to put her dream on hold to help take care of her." Danny was listening intently as she began telling the story.

"My mother went to Tennessee State when grandma was a teacher at the all black segregated Burt High School. Even though grandma expressed education first and for most, momma loved to run. When she started college and became a member of the women's track team running with some great ones on the record setting relay team. The two had grown up and went to high school together. Sketter as she was called was a sickly child who had been stricken with polio wearing a brace on one of her legs. My mother was the strong one when it came to running and playing while the two of them were girls. She helped encourage her best friend to take those braces off, exercise her legs, body and run. After a while the two of them were always together playing all sports and competing and beating boys in many of them. They both came to Tennessee State making the women's track team and became the two star runners. Just before the Olympic trials my mother was diagnosed with lupus, a devastating diseases that causes severe pain throughout your body I mean every muscle and fiber of your body aces. She had to quit the team just as Sketter qualified for the Olympic team. My mother was crushed because that was her dream too. Her best friend told my mother that sense she had helped in her time of need that she would hold off on Olympic trials for a time to help her get well. Momma was furious she told her that regardless what happened to her she was not going to let her friend Sketter lose out on her dream of being an Olympic champion. Momma told her 'You got to do this for the both of us' Which she did going on to win three gold medals more than any other woman had ever won in one sport. My mother died not long after she had me then I came to live with my grandparents. She and Sketter stayed friends right up until the end momma being just as proud as if she had won those medals that was her victory. I shared that story with you to let you understand that your mother wants you to go on because this is your turn to for fill your dream and if she is anything like my mother was when you win that gold it will make her so proud because it will be a victory for her too. Danny leaned over kissing her on the forehead. "Woman you are incredible, Thanks I needed to hear that; I am going to call my mother right now and let her know I have won myself a good woman and I am going on to win the gold.

At that moment Billy was hugging him in jubilance snapping him back to reality. "We did it Danny we won the Gold Medal!!" The roar from the stands was deafening as thousands of camera lights flickered and flashed in the crowd. Danny with tears could not speak. He only waved the American Flag high over his head saying to himself "Momma, My Dad, Doris, T Man, Uncle Ike and even my great—great grand—dad that old run—away slave. This one is for all of you, for you were the ones who were behind me and holding me up giving wings to my feet and this great victory for us all.

CHAPTER 4

LOST LAMBS

The young man stood peering out the window on the second floor of an abandoned building with fear then anger in his youthful but hardened eyes. He was like a cat, ever so quiet, motionless and alert watching the events unfold in the run down house across the street. He cursed silently while the police herded his crew into their patty-wagon all handcuffed and chained. The boy flinched when the insensitive officers crammed and threw his friends inside as if they were no more than a pack of rats, while silently being glad he wasn't among the group. He thought to himself, there is Jo Jo, whom he met in kindergarten. The boys played tag and hide& seek on the high rise project stair— where both lived. The first time he and Fish met they got into a fight but not long after the dust settled the boys became friends. In many cases this was the way you got to know your homeboys, provided you weren't killed, in their hood. The teen gritted his teeth after one of the officers slammed Lonnie's head into the side of their vehicle for moving to slow. He thought about the times they stopped in front of the Maple sisters unit hoping to impress them with their rap routine and Ray-Ray, his "dog" was always there in case he had to get it on with some of his rivals at school. In the projects children needed a friend to watch their backs in and out of school at all times.

As a matter of fact the boys formed an alliance, a brotherhood, or club for that very reason like musketeers each vowed one for all and all for one, bonded together no matter what price had to be paid. Because for the most part each boy was the only real family the other had. Many grown-ups were either chasing that elusive high all day, or working long hours on menial jobs. The parenting of children was virtually non-existent. The children raised each other off the knowledge and skills they obtained in the streets. Those cold, hard, deadly and unforgiving streets: The dope men, pimps and hustlers were their idols and greatly admired, because they were the only ones who seemed to be 'getting paid' This scenario has been played so often until it's almost as repetitive and dull as a broken record to some. Yet the fact still remains that thousands of young lives are being wasted and lost every-day for following the 'paper trail.' Jails are becoming the main and fastest growing housing units in many cities. Everyone from small children on up know how important those <u>dead presidents</u> are. Too many young people are willing to adopt the wrong life-style to get them. They won't realize until it's too late that they are on the road of no return where the ends is, jail, institutions or death. The lambs shall surely lose their way without love and guidance.

And these lambs became 'wolves.' They grew into cunning street wise and hardened hustlers; who carved them a spot on those streets, building an enterprise off selling drugs. The young boys were known throughout the projects, in Boston's inner city as the *Chili Mack's.* A notoriously infamous gang of teens who ran their dope trade like a well-oiled machine; distributing their product to runners, who sold it to customers. There were those in the gang whose primary job was to make sure the supply kept up with the demands. Some were responsible for taking care of the bank (money). And of course there were some in security; who made sure no one tried to infringe upon their turf or confiscated their contraband.

The brains behind this operation was; T. *Man*, a lad who made friends easily and absorbed knowledge like a sponge, except in school, where he lost interest at age 12. He and his main 'Dog' or 'Homeboy', Andre, the quiet no non-sense enforcer 'took no prisoners', building an operation serving their customers with the 'quickness' but deadly if someone got in the way. Most everyone on the 'stroll' and in the projects knew not to tangle with the *Chili Mack's.* But any-time you're king of the hill, sure as day turns into night someone is going to try and knock you off.

The ones who would be kings were a rival gang in the projects on the other side of Mass Ave. This crew was known as the *Center Diamonds*, who had designs on setting shop upon the *Mack's Turf*. So the stage was set for a confrontation with the winner taking control, all profits and all the bragging rights of an area filled with addicts, dope fiends, crack heads, and winos. It came down to what was like the shoot-out an all-out war between rival factions, like soldiers fighting for the high ground, and when the smoke cleared two diamonds bite the dust and Andrea lay dying in the moon-lite night. Most scattered throughout the projects while some went back to their units to collect their goods. And for the first time since T. Man was twelve he shed tears, because it was all he could do for his 'Dog'. It was later upon arriving back at the hang-out; police were hauling the rest of his crew away, and soon would be looking for him. So he crept quietly out the back door of the building. You see self-preservation is the first law of nature in this jungle.

The teen struck out down Mass. Avenue desperation in his eyes and a 9MM in his jeans. He needed cash fast to lay low awhile, or better yet get out of town. He stopped at a vacant lot, sitting on a milk crate to sort things out. He watched some winos argue over a bottle; things hadn't always been like this. Oh how he used to love this neighborhood as a boy. After moving from city to city as a small boy his father finally settled his family in the Roxbury section of Boston's inner city. He later learned that his father packed them all up and left Chicago in a hurry after the leader and spokesman for his organization was killed in the pre-dawn raid for which the police and F.B.I. agents said they were looking for weapons when they were fired upon.

During the late 1960's the protest movement was becoming violent with anti-government and anti-war rallies being held from college campuses, to what was being called anarchy in city streets, even disrupting the Democratic National Convention in Chicago. Civil rights leaders and spokesman of the people, who were crying for equality and justice, weren't merely being arrested but, 'executed' right in front of America on National T.V. It was becoming a total breakdown of society and Revolution seemed on the horizon after Dr. King then Robert Kennedy was murdered. J. Eager Hoover's covert-war called cointelpro hunted down those who spoke out against anything the government was doing and took no 'prisoners'. This especially meant organizations like the Black Panthers that had spread from Coast to Coast. The group of militant young black's started by two young outspoken young black men, had chapters in every major city in the United States.

T.Man's father was a member of the Chicago Chapter, where he was in charge of the newly formed 'school breakfast program' for a school on the cities Southside. His two young children would be attending that elementary school soon and he along with other group members realized that before a child's mind could be developed and feed education their bodies had to be feed food. Too many children went to school hungry. So the mothers would get up early in the morning to prepare breakfast for children's schools in their communities, then the organizations fathers would distribute them hot and ready to the kids every morning before class. His interest and main reason for joining was to make sure poor children like his had an equal chance of succeeding. This program started by the Panthers for *inner city* children worked so well, and was in such great demand that it was adopted by the Federal Government becoming a National Platform for all elementary schools across the United States.

The positive reasons got lost as the desperation by the 'Law and Order' proponents voices grew louder. The 'powers that be' were determined that the leaders of the dangerous radical groups that were, as Hoover had labeled them, "The greatest threat to American security" had to be eliminated where ever they could be found to prevent a 'messiah' from emerging to organize and lead all these radical and militant groups and mount a serious challenge to the present system of government in the United States. The Viet Nam war was already going badly after the Tet-Offensive, so they could not afford to lose the battle in the hearts and streets of Americans. After the Panther leadership were killed in the pre-dawn raid on Chicago's West Side. Brother Jackson, T. Man's father, took his wife and their two children and fled to Cleveland, later Buffalo and then finally ending up in Boston with the hope of a new life.

There are many things in one's life that can't be predicted and we can plan events in our lives much as we want but not the outcome. Growing up in Roxbury started out as a good life for a young adventurous boy. So it was for Thomas, Andre, and the rest of the 'homes'. The boy thought about the times they used to play ball in this very lot as children. His mind went back to the times after their game when they would ride their bikes to Smithy's Sweet Shop. Closing his eyes he could still smell those rolls, bread, donuts, and cakes being baked in the neighborhood bakery. Every kid in the projects knew old man Smithy. He gave loaves of bread, donuts, cakes, and bags of candy on holidays to the needy families.

The old bakery owner loved children, he and his wife had lost theirs. They too had escaped, barely getting out of Poland in time during the Nazi occupation of their homeland. Their two children were not as fortunate. The boy and his sister were shipped off to a Concentration Camp as a result of the Warsaw Ghetto uprising. Both parents arrived in America with just the cloths on their backs but lucky to be alive and in the land of the 'Free' they know all too much about despair, strife, and the hardships people in the community were subjected to; most being on welfare, fixed incomes or just unable to find a decent job. T.Man could still hear his older sister after roller skating up to the shop looking for him. "Thomas, mama want you to come home right now." He and Andre would ride their bikes along the L. tracks through those girders on the way back home.

How happy life was back then, that is until one horrifying day when he was about twelve-years old. His father had worked hard, saved his money and bought him a taxi-cab wanting to have his own business and be his own boss. On most weekend nights, which was his busiest, he would drive for twenty hours straight before going home to take a break. On this particular night he had picked up what would be his last passenger, who convinced the driver to stop at a store before delivering him to his destination. All of a sudden two shots rang out in the still of the night as the passenger jumped out the cab and ran down the street. T. Man's father was left slumped over the wheel with two bullet holes in the back of his head, and cab still running.

It seemed like at that moment a sharp pain went through his wife's heart as the feeling of dread and doom consumed her whole being. She always had a bad feeling about him driving 'that cab' unnecessarily exposing him-self to danger and the target of those forces that were responsible for them having to leave Chicago. When the phone rang she let out a screams "Oh god no, Why? God Why?" Her friends and neighbors tried to console the hysterical sobbing women. The E.M.S. people on the other end of the line were giving her some details about what happened. By the time they had taken him out of his Taxi-Cab the man had sarcoma to the two gunshot wounds that were caused by a small caliber hand gun, one entering the back of his neck and the other the base of his head. The two officers who came by the house informed her that they could only assume it was robbery because his log book with the number of passengers, pick-ups and destinations was gone with the receipt book and receipts'.

When Thomas arrived at his house; the boy pushed through neighbors and saw his mother crying on the floor. He looked at her with mouth gaped in complete shock as a neighbor turned to him. "Thomas, it was your father, he dead". "No why he leave me, we was supposed to go camping in the summer?" as tears began streaming down his cheeks. God, he loved that man. Right then and there the hopes and dreams of a son spending time with his 'dad' had died, as he became an 'orphan of the revolution'. Many historians surmised that after the militant and radical generation of the 1960's was eliminated there was a void left in its place, to be filled. This void was filled with what is now called the gang-bangers, thugs or street gangs that sprang up from coast to coast. Instead of taking up the cause of justice and inequality in the inner city streets as their fathers, uncles, older brothers and even mothers had done they took on the cause of 'just give me mine' and will use any means necessary to get mine from any-body I can get it from. The hard drugs from Southeast Asia began to flood the streets, as deadly weapons of every description became the easiest commodity to obtain in the inner cities with guns being turned inward on the 'community'. The militant organizations black and white stopped talking about 'the revolution 'or 'power to the people' and 'black power' especially after its leaders were either in jail or like his father dead.

"Hey don't drink all the dam wine". T. Man wiped his eyes focusing on the two men still arguing over the bottle, coming back to reality. For a few moments he was in a dream world, he wanted things to be the way they were before his father died. But, this looking around is the way life really is Wino's fighting over a bottle, his idol dead, T. Man's mother became an alcoholic spending most of her time in mental institutions. His sister in the streets selling her body to support a drug habit, Andre dying, old man Smutty gone. He dropped out of school looking for love and some kind of family. Then society condemns his way of life, but they don't really care. Besides, what else is there of life but violence, poverty, pain and one trap after another waiting on your every step. Well he knew one thing for sure.

The only thing that counted was them 'dead presidents. The only way to get yours was to be the most cunning and deadly animal in the jungle he reasoned.

T. Man took the 9 mm glock from his jeans, checking to make sure he had a full clip then got up proceeding down the street. He walked four blocks thinking, I need some dead presidents. He finally stopped and walked into a 7-eleven "Is that all son", T. Man nodded and when the man was about to ring up the purchase, he stepped back pulling the gun out of the jeans The guy was startled, his eyes widened and lips trembled. "All right dude check in them presidents don't try no tricks and you won't get hurt." The guy was startled his eyes widened and lips trembled. A man and two women were shopping, so with pistol aimed he signaled for them to lie on the floor "Put your hands on the back of your head, noses to the floor, and I mean if anyone breaths I'll blow your heads off." The people were petrified and silently praying the young man wouldn't pull the trigger. Hands shaking the cashier filled a bag with money. "Now get down on the dam floor and don't move." The cashier lay behind his counter; T.Man grabbed the bag and headed out the door.

At that moment two police officers had just finished eating at the pizzeria three doors down and about to get into their squad car. Suddenly T. man stepped out into the street gun in one hand bag of money in the other. The officers looked up with complete surprise to see the gun wheeling teen. Both pulled weapons from their holsters. T. Man upon spotting them whirled ready to break wide in the other direction. "Halt police!" Drop that gun or we'll shoot." The officer seemed to plead. The boy with a frightened look and tears in his eyes squeezed the trigger. Both officers ducked behind their cars raised up and returned fire hitting the boy in his chest. The bag of money flew one way, his weapon the other. People screamed as T. Man grabbed his chest being knocked back by the impact then falling on the curb not moving. One officer went to call E.M.S, the other policeman ran over to him, "Why didn't you just drop the gun son?" T. Man was D.O.A at the same hospital his homeboy died in the night before. And the lambs shall surely lose their way without love and guidance.

T. Man's father, Brother Jackson, had once made some dire revelations and predictions just before they left Chicago that seemed to have come to pass. Besides being instrumental in helping to organize the children's breakfast program he mentored and lectured young teens about future hazards that might be-fall them. "I see it coming just on the horizon not many days away" he said as if gazing into a crystal ball. "That Mr. 1970 will be here and when he does show up he will look at our streets, neighborhoods, community and inner city and say what has happened here? I see a place that had been teaming with life, love, prosperity, and true concern for thy neighbors. The movement of the 1960's brought forth a new dawn and new day by men's visions and dreams. Mr. 1970 walked through the streets and all he could see were the broken shattered remnants of ideas, plans and dreams, of the well—intended. He will view the remains of the leaders that made those inspiring speeches (Dr. King, Malcolm X, Robert Kennedy and Fred Hampton.) whose voices have been silenced forever and say All seems Lost and for not.

As darkness blankets the land Mr. 1970 will see in the shadows a figure lurking through the night. He will see a shadowy, smooth talker that goes from street to street and door to door harking. "In my bag I have the answer to all your ills and woes, a simple solution, it is something that can make you all powerful and bring wealth beyond your wildest imagination. It is the stuff for which dreams are made of. Once introduce to the lowly and disheartened, they will be at your feet for time in mortal. They will want it more than anything else, turn against anyone to have it, and kill if necessary to keep it." Yet in actually it is the weapon that shall be used to declare war on them without their knowledge, something they must have and will pit brother against brother to keep it. It won't stop there by any means. All the young ones going to either be in jail or killed by their own hand." He looked over to Mr. 1970 saying. "After the old ones die out because we going to make it impossible for them to get adequate health care that is in anyway equal. After all it would be defeating our purpose if they get the best doctors and medical care that others have to pay for. This must be done, we heard King's speech too" 'I might not get there with you' "Well we made sure he didn't, and now must make sure the Orphans of the Revolution who will look for a leader and someone to follow him, we must make sure they don't find a messiah to get them to the promised land as a people either"

As T. Man's dad finished he seemed to have stared into the great beyond or some crystal ball, the youngsters looked at him in awe, in total dismayed, and some even in shock. Yet it all came to him like a vision out of the future transcending into the here and now. "Pharaoh condemned the entire first born of his slaves the children of Israel to death, this time it seems all of our people have been condemned." A few days later he made the decision to move and make the great escape with his wife and two children. He knew full well that as a member of the Panther Party he would be a target anywhere he went, but felt it was worth the risk to give his family a chance at a new life. So like Joseph had left Egypt to escape Pharaoh's death threats in hope of something better.

He left the Orphans and just every-day kids. And many of them in big cities from L.A. to Chicago, to Detroit and New York, D.C, and Boston were left looking for someone or something to fill the void of leadership and role model.

They had been abandon and deserted in despair, and now were frustration, anger and confusion. They longed for guidance, direction, protection, and a sense of belonging. So they formed gangs that they would hope make them feel like being a part of family whom they could count on and trust. What they didn't count on or know about was that as part of the government's covert operation they would be targeted under assault and attack by a new and sinister weapon of war that they never envisioned. The fire of rebellion was being extinguished by the same means that the British Empire had used in their Opium Wars and Chinese Boxer Rebellion.

This time however it was Opium and Heroin from Southeast Asia, which was once French Indochina, allowed to flow into the inner city mostly black communities. Coming from that golden triangle and same area that Danny's father and so many other young Americans had fought and died to protect and liberate. It is very ironic and worth noting that if all those drugs were not allowed to flow then someone left the door wide opened and unguarded while death and destruction slipped in. Like a giant seven headed dragon that came up out of the sea followed by a tsunami that drenched the land drowning most in its wake in order to bring about *Law and Order for a New Order* to be created. Little did T. Man's dad realize that his son along with so many of that lost and displaced would be sweep up and washed a-way along with it?

CHAPTER 5

A CLOCK UNWINDS

It was a clear crisp autumn day and the sun sparkled brightly high in the sky, with only a Wisk of clouds in the brilliant blue heavens. A brisk Northwest breeze shook branches of the trees, which gave up; their bounty of leaves, re, amber, gold and orange leaves fluttered in the wind; down, down, then playfully running through the grass like children spinning round, and chasing one another until they all disappeared each going their separate way, As an old man sat on the park bench listlessly watching the entire episodes unfold before his engaging glance.

He wore a faded tweed overcoat with a broken down hat covering his thinning gray hair. As he gazed around a smile came upon his bearded face. About ten yards directly in front of him two teenage boys were scampering about. "Hey man, you threw that one too high." One complained. "Yea, well I forgot you ant no Jerry Rice that could run, leap, and catch it!" The other barked. The wobbly pass missed its mark, bouncing end over end toward the bench, landing at the old man's feet. Without hesitation he reached down gripping the ball with one hand. The errant quarterback ran over to the bench reaching hands out as the old man looked up grinning. "It's all in the grip, son put your fingertips on the stiches of the football, holding it tight, square your shoulders, plant your throwing foot." As the man stood he was gesturing. "Then step into the pass letting go with arm and wrist."

The other boy ran impatiently up to his friend. Come on Jimmy; get the ball from that old man so we can finish practicing." But Jimmy was engulfed listening to his instructor who seemed to know what he was talking about the old man flipped the ball to Jimmy. "Try and see if it will work for you." The boy stepped to the side, gripping the ball and going through every detail the old man had instructed as he motioned for his friend to go out for pas the boy cradled the ball on his finger-tips. Jimmy turned to the old man. "How do you know so much about football?" The man started grinning revealing dingy teeth. "Well, son if you got a couple of minutes, I'll tell you a story." Jimmy sat next to him while his impatient friend stood listening. "This ball was a part of my life far back as I can remember, my whole life revolved around it or it had an effect on choices I made." The old man's mind began to unwind as he revealed his many yester-years.

"It was right after the assassination of President Kennedy the nation went from shock to mourning, going through life in disbelief. It was the end of Camelot, but the beginning of a new life for me. We had moved to a middle class neighborhood, away from the 'Bottom' we live in, just before I was to start high school. Everything was clean, fresh, and exciting, besides the fact that we didn't have to look at the stars while taking a bath. I still remember the first day I met my new friends Matthew, and a group of guys who were standing together. It seems we were members of the few African American families that dotted the neighborhood. Mathew was a tall kid with leadership skills like you." The boy stuck his chest out. "Anyway one of the guys blurted out." "Hey man when we going up to the play-ground and take it away from them white boys, they act like it's all theirs and we got much right to play there as they do?" "You right but we ant going to have to fight with no knives, chains, or baseball bats, I made a deal with their leader for us to get up a football team to play a no holes bared game with them and if we win we gonna be able to play when we want, but if they win we gonna have to go some-where else and play ball. So get all the guys you can together." For the first time he paid me some attention. "Hey new guy can you play tackle football and do you want to play on our team?" Standing toe to toe with him. "My name is Isaac and yea I will play on your team." Looking me up and down he asked. "You any good." I reached out my hand. "Just give me the ball."

During the mid-1960's integration in the North had just begun along with the movement in the South to tear down the walls of segregation. The area we had moved to although mixed still had its boundaries and boarders. The Main Avenue was the dividing line in which on one side were a scattered few African American families and on the other side there were no minorities families what so ever. Our school along with playground and park was on the side where all the white families stayed, and although the school was integrated they felt like the playground and all its facilities belonged to them therefore we were expected to run back to our side of the 'tracks' after school, and just be content that we could go to 'their school'. Of course we weren't standing for that, and with tensions at a fever pitch, were on the verge of not only a racial confrontation, but like in the movie 'West Side Story' a rumble over what we believed was our right, to go where and when we pleased in the neighborhood. The decision had been made, just before I met Mathew and his boys, to settle the dispute on the playground with a football rather than knives, baseball bats, chains, and fist.

The boys gathered their team together and headed for the playground. The other team were members were standing in the middle of the football field waiting. A red headed Irish kid named Patrick Edwards was their team leader as he nodded to Mathew, one of his guys blurted. "I guess them 'Sambos' can count to eleven after all, they got the right amount of guys." The guys on his side broke into laughter. This caused one of our fellows to remark. "I wonder if you momma taught you to count to twelve when I start doing the dozens on you 'Honkie." Some of the boys on each side began to get riled and up into the others face, as Mathew and Patrick had to restrain their teams. "Hold on fellows we will settle this on the field." After the kick off it was on, the game being like a tug of war match going back and forth. Both the boys were good at quarterbacking and the game was tied in the final minute. In our last huddle Mathew told me that he was going to fake a pass and hand the ball off to me and I better run for the touch—down. "No problem man just give me the ball and a couple blocks and those six points are in the bag. He faked it and I ran an end around for 25 yards and the winning score." Our team jumped for joy hugging and shaking my hand, as our counterparts head down walked away dejected.

Not only did we win the right for us to play on the school playground but all the other African American kids on our side of the Avenue could have access to it along with us a somewhat uneasy truce was forged between both races as a result of. All the kids could enjoy playing on the lush green play-ground, and were able to cross the invisible boarder that had been the wide Main Avenue could play, making their neighborhood truly an integrated one. The uneasy truce forged between both races led to a healthy respect for one-another's ability on the field and a determination to come out on the winning end.

Many of the boys who played the game on that field that early spring day ended up at the same integrated high school competing against one another to win position on the newly integrated football team. Some became friends, a few adversaries, and still others inter squad rivals. No matter what side their feeling fell on all had come away with that same attitude of not wanting to let the other person out do them after that famous big game on the field of the neighborhood playground on that warm spring day.

Isaac, Mathew, and Patrick were among those who became friends with many calling them the 'Oreo Brothers', the two dark colored ones with the cream colored one in the middle. The boys also were examples for many of the younger kids who saw the fact that whites and blacks could live and play together in peace and harmony, being comfortable with one another's company while also becoming good friends in the process. It was a great learning experience for the whole community. Asides from that, all three had designs on making the high school football team, spending all day for the most part up at the play-ground honing their skills.

The boys were on their way home stopping to toss the ball back and forth. Matthew seeing Patrick was better at quarterbacking started using his long frame to be a sure handed wide receiver, but there was no doubt that all three had a personal goal of making the school football team. They spent time over one another's house sharing and getting to know each-others families, and always together. Summer practice was posted and all the potential and want a be's signed up for team and hit the field. The coach was a task master as he scheduled the two a day practice sessions making sure they were drilled and drilled on the basics of the game, and all that running which was followed by body building with the weights. Later came the pads, helmets and the hard hitting, blocking and tackling.

After summer practice ended with its grueling workout, all of them were called together. The assistant coach read off the names of the guys who made the squad. The coach pulled Isaac, Matthew and Patrick off to the side. "I admire your spirit and enthusiasm, but I'm going to red shirt you and a few others who I feel have potential but need more time to work on your skills, then by next year when some of these guys graduate, you'll be ready." All three walked away vowing to become the best at their positions. Patrick was the accurate throwing quarterback, Matthew the sure handed wide receiver, and Isaac the quick nimble footed running back. They studied over one another's house, and practiced to sharpen their skills, rain, shine, sleet or snow, it was them and that foot-ball. By their senior year the others had graduated and they were top players, on a top rated team that was ready to play for the cities championship.

It was on the day of the game when they were to play archrival Denton High for the championship. Patrick dashed frantically up the stairs standing outside of the American History class. He nervously waited for class to end. Matthew stepped outside. "What's up man?" With worried look he pulled him aside. "Our big game is this evening and ant no sighting of Isaac." Frowning Matthew shot back. "What do you mean, I though he rode to school with you?" He did but after that I don't know what happened." Shrugging his shoulders. After interrogating each other they took off toward the gym to question Coach Williams. "Look Coach Isaac ant in school and we got that gig game this evening." Worried look on both boys faces. The Coach gave a reassuring glance. "Well Isaac's mother was rushed to the hospital, right after he got to school, and sense they haven't located his father yet, the school took him over to the hospital to be with her." Patrick joined in "What happened to his mother Coach?" "We don't know for sure, but she passed out and a neighbor called 911 and after she got to emergency the hospital called us." Matthew spoke up. "We're all in this together Coach, so we are going to the hospital right after school." Both boys were in complete agreement. "Don't you two forget that we have a game and I want you back here, for this game?"

When the boys made it to the hospital Isaac was sitting at his mother's bed side nervously holding her hand. "Momma I can't leave you no matter what else happens I will be here by your side." She looked up at the other two boys as they entered the room. You know I always had weak lungs everysense I was in that fire as a young girl. So now they think I might have Pneumonia in both my lungs." "No mamma, no I won't leave your side," As tears began to well in his eyes. Your momma going to be all-right don't worry about me I've been through much worst stuff than this, besides they finally got hold of your dad, he been doing that construction job over in the next county. This is what I want you to do for your momma; I know you got the big game today that's why your two friends are here. It is important for your momma that you get the victory that you dreamed of." She gave all of them a proud smile. "So go out there and win one for your Momma. Isaac leaned over and hugged his mother. "That's why I love you so, you the greatest. Let's go fellows we have a game to play."

They arrived in time to suit up and take the field. The stands were filled to capacity with spectators from both schools cheering, clapping hollering and whistling for their respective teams. This game was for all the marbles. They all roared with enthusiasm, and win they did. The whole team brought their A game that day. When the dust settled and both teams were totally exhausted, they came out on top. The three friends along with the team were mobbed as the Coach received his gator bath. The old man was all aglow as both boys had been listening intently. "Wow! That was some story, what was the final score?" One boy blurted out. "We beat them by two touchdowns, but the most important thing was my momma was alright and we won for her and for us."

The boys who had been listening intensively got up and resumed tossing their ball as the evening breeze rustled the trees shaking more leaves from their sleep the old man pulled out a bag and began feeding the birds with a smile on his lips as a middle-aged woman took the seat on the bench next to him. She looked somewhat puzzled as she reached in her bag pulling out one of the bright red cherries she just purchased at the fruit market. The old man, who was once that boy named Isaac, glanced in her direction, greeting her. "Afternoon mam, you know life is like a bowl of cherries some are sweet and others can be bitter." She looked at him question mark on her face. "Can I tell you what I am talking about man?" He added.

"I received a scholarship in football to KSU (Kentucky State University) while my two friends went to school in different parts of the country. We had played together in high school and thought we might be able to attend the same college, but it didn't work out as planned so I ended up in Kentucky. I made the team as the first string running back, and things were going good until I tore my A.C.L mid –way through the season as a red shirt freshman. I was devastated to say the least, because no matter how much therapy I had or how much I wanted it to heal it wasn't happening for me. At the start of the next season I didn't even make the cut and I was thinking about quitting school, going back home or joining the Army. Of course at that time there was the Viet Nam War in Southeast Asia and the Civil-rights movement was in full swing. Dr. King had completed the Selma to Montgomery voting rights march and was heading North, to what turned out as 'Battle ground Chicago'.

He thought the South was bad until he ran into some hard core Northern biggest. Dr. King remarked that he never had as much fear for his safety as he did when he was marching through one of those all white neighborhoods of Cicero, where he was cursed, harassed, spit at and even stoned by roving bands of whites. In the North Jim Crow couldn't be seen on the signs and in laws, but he was more than alive hiding behind the invisible façade of well-kept homes with velvet green neatly cut lawns and white picket fences. A lot of the old Southern traditions were coming down as the strong holds along with the die-hearts were coming around and not only integrating public facilities, but also hiring black people to good paying government jobs. So our campus was filled with recruiters from all walks of life hoping to sign people up for an array of positions.

I thought about what had happened to Dr. King in a Northern city, Chicago of all places, and wondered why there wasn't enough police security, that is black police protection around to ensure his safety. I was always fascinated with wearing a uniform, and being a part of a team. As fate would have it on my way back to the dorm I saw a recruiter that was attempting to sign people up for law enforcement positions in Southern Metropolitan Cities. The officer exclaimed "There is a big push to have black police officers that are making a difference all over the South, the public demands it and the time is right for it." I walked over to him and asking. "Which ones are you talking about?" He gave me a list and immediately Memphis Tennessee stood out, for one reason it wasn't for from my campus and of course it was not in the Deep South, I had come to the realization that my college football playing days were over. I knew it was time to turn the page and start righting a new chapter in my life, so why not a job as a law-enforcement officer.

As one of the first minority recruits at the Memphis Police Academy I had the distinct honor of being what called a 'token black' who was given a chance to join the force. And let me tell you my fellow white trainees never let me forget it. There was over four months of physical endurance, and mental anguish that made me sometimes feel that I was the target and the criminal. There was a huge auditorium that we met in to have our daily pep talks or lectures by various law-enforcement and Political officials. Then we would have breakfast in one of two 500 seat dining halls, where I usually ate alone. After which we would go to P.T (physical training), before hitting the weight room or gym. The classes were you learned the do's and don'ts of law-informant, the drivers training course, shooting range and hand to hand combat was thrown in for the good of a well—rounded officer of the law. After over 120 sessions I graduated and became one of Memphis finest or Police Cadet as the reminded me time and again. For the first time the woman sitting next to the old man seemed to pay attention to what he was saying. "You were a police officer and now you are sitting here on a bench looking like a hobo, so what happened?" Now he had and ear to tell his story.

"I was assigned to the P.S.T. (public safety technical squad). Their job was to issue citations (tickets), recover stolen vehicles, along with support and escorting certain high ranking people. I was told because of my college back ground I would be best suited for this. The main thing I saw was that didn't carry a weapon. I can only surmise at that time a token black man was not really trusted with a gun. I worked out of the Main Street Precinct Station. During my rookie year there were quite a few events that happened all over the country that had a profound effect on my-self and everybody else in this nation. Riots, as our authority called them broke out in major cities like Detroit, Newark, and parts of New York. It seemed like a revolution fueled by discontent was everywhere, marches and protest went from city streets to college campuses. The authorities scrambled to get hold of situation. It was like putting a finger in the hole in a dike only to have other leaks brake out all over. And here I was a law enforcement officer without a weapon, (a cop without a gun) how could I enforce the law like that.

An incident with the sanitation workers broke out in which they took their protest and strike to the streets. As police officer I had been sent to help make sure order was maintained. This time I had a baton, helmet, shield, and vest to go up against the striker agitators if necessary. And all they were doing was walking, carrying signs proclaiming that they wanted to be treated like men. The Mayor told them he wouldn't meet with them because their strike was illegal, ordering them back to work. He then turned to the police chief and told him if they didn't respond and got out of hand it was all right to crack some heads. We waded into them and dispersed the crowd, but they didn't go back to work. It wasn't until later that I found out the reason they were so animated about not giving in. Two workers had crawled into the back of their truck to avoid the rain and were crushed to death, but what really got me was that the reason they did this was because in certain neighborhoods they weren't allowed in businesses or residential homes, just to come out of the rain. Being from the North I had never heard of anything as absurd as this, nor did I think things like this really happened.

Then in March of 1968 one of the reasons that inspired me to join the force happened. Dr. Martian Luther King came to Memphis to join the sanitation workers cause. The least I can say is I was pretty excited that he would take time out of his busy schedule to help a bunch of garbage collectors. I had heard about him organizing the 'Poor Peoples' march in Washington D.C, yet heeded to the request of the workers to help them in their quest for equal treatment along with forming their own Union. I also know that after his debauch in Chicago and little to no success in L.A., he went to New York and delivered that controversial anti—Viet Nam war speech. He received a lot of heat for taking a stand on something that was considered a political issue; but to him it was more of a moral or human rights stand and in line with his philosophy 'non-violent'. I admired him because he had the courage to stand up for his beliefs, even though it put him at odds with the President. I believe he truly felt that men all over the world had a duty to spread peace, and good-will not war. The President was furious because he felt betrayed by this black man whom he had pushed the civil-rights legislation through for costing him most of the Southern white votes.

I.G.

At that time I really didn't have any views on segregation or integration nor did I believe that we would overcome. Far as I could see it my life and career were in limbo, because I missed the boat. After all, my two high school buddies had made things happen for themselves. Patrick became. Lt. Patrick Edwards, an officer in the U.S Army, who just shipped out to Viet Nam and fames Matthew had just signed a lucrative contract with a pro-football team on the West Coast. Here I was playing nurse maid to dignitaries when they came to town along with keeping striking workers in their place. I felt more like a glorified butler than a police officer. That's; when I began to have second thoughts about what I was doing, because I was beginning to think of myself as the 'Spook who sat by the Door' and being one of those left out of the American Dream.

There was something that stuck in my head however. Dr. King had become one of; the most extraordinary men of his time, who was awfully courageous and driven. He always advocated peaceful passive civil disobedience, which means that his weapon in fighting his war was to confront the enemy on all fronts taking all the wrath, disrespect, foul language, physical and emotional abuse, degradation and humiliation, in an orderly dignified manner, knowing his life was in constant danger. He showed by his actions, (winning the Novel Peace Prize). And he demanded it from all those who were part of his movement. Even before the mostly young protestors were put on the front line to protest they had to pass a grueling test to make sure that no matter what actions befell them taahaey would all-ways respond with non-violence. I would not have passed that test because there are only so many times I could turn the cheek. That's why I don't believe that those who became violent, braking windows, fighting, and looting were a part of his organization, even though I was on the other side wheeling the night sticks and tear gas to restore order." The women gave him a no non-sense look. "You were doing your job regardless of how you felt personally"

She ten got up and went her merry way. The old man picked up the half bag of cherries the lady had left and began to toss them in the direction of the squeals that were gathering nuts. That magnificent orange ball in the sky was slowly sinking behind the trees as the rays played peak a –boo between branches and leaves capping off a picture perfect golden day. As he soaked it in a middle aged man with brief case in hand took the seat next to him opening his case. He looked the part of someone leaving the hustle and bustle of a business day to unwind in the calm and serine of the park. "You know fall is the best season of the year with all the brilliant colors, leaves falling, and breeze blowing through the trees and sun all aglow." The man remarked as he loosened his tie and unbuttoned his suit coat. The old man exclaimed, "Yes life is even beautiful when, like fall it is coming to an end." "Oh, I hadn't thought of it like that." The business man nodded his head in agreement. "I have met a few human beings who really shinned putting on their best knowing it's the end of the road." The man looked at the old man with puzzled expression.

"I was once a Memphis Police Officer, and in 1968 was assigned to observing not only the sanitation workers that were on strike, but also Dr. King who had come to support them when the protest turned violent he left. I along with everyone else felt that was the end but he came back, and the reason why he was not going to have his name tied to any violence, he had given his word, and he was determined to resolve the issue non-violently. I thought to my—self the President has even turned his back on him, yet he refuses to give up. I later found out he was a follower of Gandhi; the mystic little man who had almost brought the British Empire to its knees. He was the spiritual leader of all the Indian people who longed for freedom, justice and equality from the English yoke. At that time India was the jewel in the crown of the British Empire that included what is now Pakistan, Afghanistan, and Burma, which at that time were all apart of India and a Colonial Empire ruled by Great Britain. Being able to rule such a vast territory with untold riches of minerals, materials, agricultural crops, well as spices of all kinds is what put the 'Great' in Britain." "Yes we all know the England ruled an Empire where the sun never set." The businessman joined in.

The old man seemed to talk in awe. "This tiny man who weaved his own simple cloths was able to convince an entire nation of ¾ of a billion mostly poor and uneducated people to go up against what was then the greatest military power in the world, using only passive resistance, and taking a complete non-violent approach as their weapon. I was a path that was far from easy as they were intimidated, beaten, tortured, and mowed down with 'Machine Guns' by the thousands for having the gal to go against English rule. Gandhi himself endured physical abuse, imprisonment, and his self-imposed hunger strides to convince his people that he would give his life for the cause. "Wasn't he murdered by one of his own people?" The business man countered. "Yes, but I believe it was ordered by the British Government. Dr. King once said a man has not lived unless there is something in his life he is willing to die for." The businessman took off his coat, reaching in his brief case taking out crumpled bag of what had been his lunch, and began tossing them on the ground giving an assortment of birds a feast. "This religious fanatic Gandhi was some kind of monk or mystic imam that wanted complete control of his people." "No!" The old man countered, "He was much more complicated than that."

I studied material on this man; Mahatma Gandhi began as a barrister, (English gentleman lawyer), who first experienced discrimination while practicing his profession in South Africa. On a business trip he had a first class pass on the train but was told that because of his color he had to ride in third class car. An argument and then physical altercation issued in which he was thrown off the train in the middle of nowhere. Right then and there he became determined to fight racial injustice no matter what the cost. Gandhi accepted the stance of non-possession for freedom and equality. This set in motion his ideal of *Satyagraha* or passive resistance, which meant a refusal to follow an unjust law. In South Arica all Indians had to have a registration document that they carried with them at all times. I was part of the law of a partied called the Black Act. Gandhi organized a community of followers who used nonviolent protest waging strikes, and refused to purchase English goods that later had the Black Act repealed. Then it was off to India and his will and determination for the freedom of all his people, Hindus', Moslems, well as the 'untouchables he stood for the freedom of all no matter the religion." The business man looked at him with a puzzled expression on his face. Didn't you tell me that you were a law enforcement officer?" He shook his head. "Yes I was very naïve then." "So what happened to change things?

"When Dr. King came back to Memphis at the request of the sanitation workers he made that prophetic speech that I believe sealed his doom. As a follower of Gandhi's passive resistance movement, knowing that the price of freedom might be death, he understood that just as the great spiritual leader of the Indian people was assinated the same might befall him before his people could over—come. He felt that just as Moses had led his people, but only was allowed to see the promise land from the mountain top; in his heart the same could be his fate. President Johnson had turned his back and favor away from the man who only a few years before said in Washington that 'We shall Overcome' in a speech before Congress himself. This was like Jobe being totally forsaken by god allowing satin to do his will and inflict great bodily harm.

I was assigned to escort, monitor, and watch his movements all the time he was there. Yet on the fateful day I was taken off my duty of watching over him at the Lorraine Motel. I became upset and taken aback when I learned a white officer took my place and two squads of other police officers were placed at readiness in the fire station as if they were expecting something to happen. I was also kept in the dark about the reason people that looked like military personal were at the station while I was being given some meniscal assignment downtown having nothing to do with the goings on at the Motel. I just remember everything and everyone being on edge. It was so much tension in the air you could cut it with a knife. One of the firemen kept looking out the window and at his watch every-other few minutes waiting for something.

An odd thing happened before I left that has stayed with me all this time." The business-man perked up out of curiosity to hear this. "One of the Police Sargent's was telling the fire Chief that they knew what time his ant rage was leaving the Motel, because the received the correct time from one of 'them' on the inside. They both laughed and it sounded as if one said 'like a turkey shoot' It was so much tension in the air that you could tell something wasn't quite right, yet no one was talking about anything. At the time my only feeling was that I had deserted my post, because I felt an obligation to be there for some odd reason. It was later while downtown that I found out that Dr. King had been shot when he stepped out of room 346 onto the Motel balcony. My heart sank as I thought to myself how could that have happened with so many public safety people around, what were fireman, and some military personnel all watching and at readiness for? Who would dare even try? It would have been insane because they could never have gotten away. I was puzzled at all the events that happened on that day April 4, 1968. Were they just watching as Dr. King was being murdered or did they orchestrate it?

About a year later my Captain called me into his office to inform me that because of my college record and dedication to the force that I was being chosen as one of the first minorities being considered for training as an F.B.I. field officer. At the time I was flattered thinking now maybe I can get my career back on track and be able to flaunt my success in front of my friends. The assignation of Dr. King and all the odd events that surrounded it had been placed on a back burner." The business-man looked at him curiously. "You said at the time like something happened to change your mind." "Well I guess you could say it was a real eye opening and mind blowing experience, when I look back, it was a real turning point in my life.

I was interviewed by the head of the F.B.I. field office in Memphis, and as he was talking he said something curious about Dr. King, he told me they had been listening to and watching every move he had made sense he got everybody riled up with his speech in Washington D.C. It occurred to me that how in the world, if they were watching and listening to him 24/7, could they have not seen or observed James Earl Ray his killer. It was then that the events surrounding his death came back. What had to be an act of fate entered helping clear up a lot of questions? Twilight was about to ascend through the trees into the park, as the business-man became all ears. "Tell me, I really want to know what happened to put a man who says he was on his way to a great career to end up on this park bench."

"During my internship I would stop in the Bar&Grill across the street from the office building. This guy came over to me who happened to be one of the agents and sat down at my table. He started talking, reveling more things about me and what was going on than I ever imagined anyone knew." Shaking hands, "I am Special Agent Frank O'Dea." Before I could respond, he injected. "And you our gift from affirmative action." The heavy set pot-bellied man with thin graying hair and a round red face, his every word came out slurred and boisterous. "Forgive me son I don't mean to be disrespectful, it's just that they ant doing you right and they didn't do him right." The man gulped down his drink and ordered another. "Can I buy you a drink while I explain what I MEANT?" Giving him a hard stare, "No drink, but I will accept an explanation." He dropped his head and slowly spoke.

"I am getting ready to retire after 30 years of service to the bureau, because at one time I enjoyed my work but now it's just too much to take." He looked up with blood shot eyes which seemed to tear up. "You may not know it but your pay for staying out of the way was to be promoted to the bureau. They couldn't have you watching while they were putting plans into motion." Giving him a look, as if he was speaking a foreign language, "Watching what?" I countered becoming irritated. "Make no mistake son everything is done for a reason and there is a plan and purpose behind it all. You were given another job assignment to get you out of the way and then they kicked you up stairs so you will keep your mouth shut." Snarling, "What you talking about, you just drunk." "I might have had a little too much to drink but I know what I am talking about. Let me tell you a story about the undeclared war.

"Your Dr. King to certain people in high positions was no more than a rabble-rouser, who was going around stirring up trouble and radical militants so that they could start revolutions and tears this country apart. Many viewed him as a danger to the security of the United States, who at least was a hypercritic, the preferable wolf in sheep cloths. To some, possibly even the Anti-Christ that is for-told in the bible. He was that silver tongue devil that chassed women, smoked cigarettes, all under the disguise of being a savior of his people. It wasn't just the Klan that called him Martin Luther 'Coon'. His every move was watched, along with all those around him especially after his speech in Washington, 'I have a dream and we shall overcome.' President Johnson finally woke up and realized he was being had so it was decided then that sooner or later he would have to be stopped. He once had those Kennedy's in his back pocket. The main one that was of concern was Bobby the Attorney General he was the one with the brains, who was persuading his brother to change the laws in favor of the hordes of blacks that were going to invade and take over good law abiding whites' way of life. He was more feared and despised by some more than his brother. Once they had things going their way in the South then they would sweep North, East, and finally west until they had the entire country turned up-side down. And let me tell you about those two brothers who ran Washington for a short-time.

The Kennedy brothers along with the lying King were the worst kind of enemies to certain elements within the Government, including very high ranking officials. The two Harvard educated spoiled rich boys whose father gave them anything they wanted, were the focus of many who became obsessed with envy and hatred. To those, especially in organized crime, their father wasn't anything but a glorified bootlegger, who paid some of their mobster friends to have his playboy son elected as President. So now the both of them one being appointed by his brother as the Attorney General, and the other one not even a real President who hid women in closets and storerooms all over the white house want to give our country away. If we let the black race have their way we might as well have a bunch of gorillas running things, was the talk in many circles of some Intelligence Offices. Let's face it the dark races don't know how to live among each other let lone run this great nation that our founding fathers started and the white race built. It was our Manifest Destiny to make the United States of America a country which stretches from sea to shining sea. And the white race is meant to rule it long as we exist, America will be ours to control." I looked at him with a combination of disdain and disbelief, was there really people who felt like he described, or was this rambling of a disturbed mind. As if senses my confusion he added.

Of course this is the mind-set of a secretive few power players behind the scene. Not all those in the Agency are of this belief, but we are sworn to secrecy and have to carry out orders or be fired and possibly never work anywhere again or yet even be imprisoned. The bull-dog who is the director of one Agency and the pipe-smoker who once headed up the other Agency are possibly the two most feared and powerful men in the country and between the two of them there isn't anything that they don't know about anyone world-wide. And if they haven't got it in hand they have excess to all the resources and connections to find out. Absolute power and control is the way they play their game. They build files on everyone no one is beyond their reach." Startled I replied. "You mean they have more power than the President?" The agent spoke carefully. "Look the President has only temporary power that he must pass onto another person, probably from another party with different views.

These are men whose power are lasting and have gone on for decades that reach back in the past and like 'octopus tenicates' to all governments past and present world—wide and will be here in the future." I was stunned, and then it hit me. "You mean, no they couldn't have had anything to do with John Kennedy and Dr. Kings death?" He paused then spoke matter of fact. "The Vice-President and the Law and Order guy were at this huge ranch right side of Dallas that can be likened to the one on that T.V. show. They were the guest of one of those Texas billionaires along with several other wealthy 'oil men'. The Bull-Dog was secretly flown in landing at a private airport on the morning of November 21. He left on that same plane for Washington D.C. late that night. Everyone knows what happened in Dallas on November 22 that next day. Many of the Secret Service people had gone to a wild party the night before at a strip club, where the liquor flowed freely. Many of the ones that didn't get drunk the night before road on the running board, and were told their job was to protect the President, but it was on the running board of the second car of the motor cade not the first car.

That day in Dallas November 22, 1963 was to be the 'Big Event', and the beginning of the New World Order with other planned events to come later. And, of course the end of Camelot along with marking the end of the 'dream'. Shaking my head. "Why and how could they think they could,? The blurry eyed man intervened. "Nothing happened by chance the plat was talked about then went into action after the March on Washington. Other plans will be put into action soon." Not wanting to believe any of it. "What plans you talking about?" The red faced man got up looking around, and then nervously spoke. "I've talked too much now, as time goes by you'll find out, all I can say is there are people like me who don't like any of it, who are powerless to do anything, that is the main reason why I am retiring this fall."

Darkness was about to invade the park area as the street light directly above their bench came on. The old man had been sitting on there unwinding the events of the past that had shaped his life which helped end him on this park bench. The business man straightened his tie and buttoned his suit coat as he was about to stand. The old man gently held his arm and said. "Let, me tell you about the other 'events' in which the agent predicted would come to past. As we all know Robert Kennedy was killed right after he won the California Primary, right in Mr. Law and Order's, home state and was going to the Democratic Convention in Chicago. By all accounts he would have been nominated to run for President. My theory after listening to that Agent is that the last thing certain forces wanted to face was the idea of losing to another Kennedy in the Presidential Election, after all Bobby was the real brains behind the Kennedy 'Brothers'. There is little doubt if he was nominated that he would have beat out Mr. Law and Order himself. After he lost to John Kennedy in 1960 he ran for California Governor, lost that election in 1962 and was politically dead, that is he couldn't have been elected as a dog catcher, yet in 1968 he not only becomes the GOP candidate but he manages to win and become President a mere six years later. It was a miraculous feat to say the least and something almost impossible in politics. Or was there some unseen force at work, something sinister that manipulated 'events' to eliminate the competition."

The business man relaxed back on the bench giving him a startled look. "Things like that just don't happen in America." The old man looked him directly in his eyes. "If you know about Karma, which is what goes around comes back around, and then think about this. Mr. Law and Order became President and broke more laws than anybody. What is ironic was the thing that cost him the Presidency was trying to cover up the break in that his men, who were paid to stop leaks by stealing files from the Democratic. You have to ask yourself what were they really after, and was the information in those files so explosive that four lifetime professionals who had done work in many Intelligence operatives, had to risk it all to break in and steal. All this to win and retain power and control. If it had not been for the cover-up to buy the burglars off the American people would never have known about it.

It was during this time that all the dirty tricks and tactics of the agency and those that had run it latterly turned my stomach. I became desponded at the entire system, as I turned my back and walked away from that kind of career. In my mind I had been living a lie and had been too much a coward to face reality. There were so many that had sacrificed and lost their lives to make a change, but were held by people like myself, who were some of the very ones they struggled to set free. But just like the agent in the bar told me, there is a price that must be paid for going against the system. Things really got bad for me when Stevey Wonder and other leaders campaigned to have Dr. King's birthday declared a National Holiday. Of course I was right in the middle of the protest, deciding this was my chance to finally stand up for what I believe was right I was one of those that went to jail along with Stevey when we picketed in front of the Capitol building. That was the entire agency needed to blackball me from going into law informant any-where at any level in the United States. Despite what happed to me we could claim a victory when the third Monday in January became a National Holiday in honor of Dr. Martin Luther King Jr.

I then went from one job to another trying to find a fit. I even became a consular for at risk teens. It felt good to be a guide to a generation of lost souls. They were like the children of Israel that were wondering in the wilderness with no real leader or clear purpose to show them the way. I once heard a guy in Boston make a speech where he claimed to be a former Black Panther way they were the 'Orphans of the Revolution.' My former employers found out where I was employed and put pressure on them and they had to discharge me. I became distraught, frustrated, angry, and depressed. As I wallowed in self-pity the bottle became my companion and friend. It seemed like the only thing I did right was to get married before getting fired, but after that happened I even shut her out. I soon ended up living in shelters, then about two years ago I was introduced to A/A where I've been trying to get my life back on track every-since." The business man looked at the 'Old Man' in a completely different light. He began to see him as the soldier that had fought in a war and after the victory and all the fanfare was left alone. The hero that time had passed by and it seemed the world had forgotten.

He handed him one of his cards saying "Get in touch with me soon my company is partner with a placement organization that may be able to find a fit for you, helping to get you back in the middle of the mainstream." The old man took the card smiling, "God works in strange ways through people who can be a complete stranger when you first meet them. But do you know what I would really like finding out about and possibly having some impact in." He looked up as if he was transporting himself to another place among the stars. Every sense Dr. King was killed that horrible day in Memphis April 4, 1968 I have been in search of the real reason 'why' and after talking to others who felt like I did, have come up with this chilling theory." The business man was all ears again wondering what the old man saw in those stars.

"There has been a war going on right here in this country, not from an outside invading force but from within. Violence was exploding in all the major cities, across the United States, on College Campuses, in small town's unrest, and in our courts changes and discontent. Many in high positions felt America was being taken over by hostile rebellious and dangerous forces. They came to the conclusion that something had to be done and like Malcolm X once said 'by any means necessary.' We must remember that they were already fighting a war in Viet Nam so it was a war on 'two fronts'. Those with the power took it on like a military campaign, to take back America and the American way of life from enemies foreign or 'domestic.' These people were earnest, sincere, and committed. It was like 'Operation Overlord' that the Allied forces used to take Europe back from the Germans. Most of the knowhow and focus was used in the taking back of the cities, colleges, courts, and towns. The same as the Generals focused everything on D. Day and storming the beaches of Normandy France. The main difference is that they could not use regular Army, Marine, and Naval troops for this war, it was tried when what they called 'riots' broke out, which really weren't riots but gorilla war fare that young people of all races and colors, were waging for their ideals.

I was told that it was 'Operation Bull'ock' (young bull male). Back in Biblical days they would take the young male and castrate him to make it less fearsome, defiant, and hostile, the objective to make them submissive and docile.

There were two main weapons the plan called for using. In the war in Southeast Asia they already had access to one weapon, the products of the 'Poppy Fields' that could not only be used to put out the fire of rebellion, but could also turn some of those defiant rebels into something like mercenary troops who they could use." The business man was in dismay as he rubbed his chin completely puzzled. "It's like this, after the weapon from that poppy plant had been spread throughout this nation's hot spots, certain places that were a major threat, places like Detroit, Chicago, Newark, New York, Las Angles, New Orleans etc. that the battle started. There was a gangster from Harlem who had contacts and received his heroin from the growers over there and he only supplied Harlem, a much more sophisticated network was at work to supply the other cities. it became the same as a military campaign. They stormed the beaches of Normandy to take back Europe now it became necessary to storm the streets of the inner cities, for seizing and controlling the enemy's strong hold. They turned the enemy against one another by using many to deliver its weapon (heroin that is extracted from the poppy) to destroy the will of their own, then turn on one-another for power, profits, and control over what had become the new battle fields. Today you can walk through the heart of most major cities that saw unrest and see it truly does look like a war zone." The business man became irritated. "Wait a minute, there is no way you can convince me the U.S. Government declared war or anything like that on its own citizens, no matter what color they may be."

The old man looked him straight in the eyes. "There are two things I want you to take under consideration. I am not saying that the men who have the power and make the decisions for our Nation came up with this plan or conspiracy. There are those in Government and outside, who have the leaderships ear and who they confide in and trust in making decisions; some have been persuasive enough to convince them that the events of the day where the sons of former slaves are a threat to the sons of former slave masters, (there were many slave revolts during those times, that took many lives white and black). The master biggest fear was his slaves coming in the middle of the night to take what they wanted before raping and killing him and his family. When the decedents of those slaves took to the streets taking what they wanted, terror gripped the decedents of the masters as they were ready to come up with any drastic action to save family and home. The next thing I want you to realize is that this nation was truly on the verge of a Revolution, the secret weapon (drugs) and the secret war. (cointelpro) subdued that.

I.G.

And what was left was the 'Orphans of the Revolution' who like lost lambs left wandering." The business man countered matter of fatly. "So I guess you going to tell me that was an excuse for them committing crimes, robbery, murder and whole sale mayhem." "There is never any excuse for that, but there is a reason."

He paused for a long second then continued. "Self-preservation is the first law of nature for any animal in the jungle be it in Viet Nam or the 'Asphalt Jungles in cities streets. Orphans are those children who have lost family and home. Too many of them were the children of the casualties, mainly their fathers and male family role models. The mothers, strong women that they were, had been left alone to protect, provide for and raise them in single parent homes. The family which is the basis of any community is more than one parent with her children. It takes a father along with a (village) to look after and raise the young 'bull' sons. You have heard athletes and many in show business say that they are lucky because they made it 'out'. What they are talking about is they made it out of the 'hood' that has become a trap in-which too many youth were caught up in. The fathers who abandoned their sons were lured into a life of violence, drugs, despair or just lost hope. Many didn't know or care that their sons and sons, sons along with so many other children would be born into a cycle of violence, destruction, drugs and death. The lambs shall surly lose their way without love and guidance, so they became entrapped and led to the slaughter. Those that didn't make it out of the trap were reduced to animal level to survive, becoming hungry wolves, preying on everything and everybody. And of course they were supplied by rouge arms dealers and organized drug dealers with the tools they need to destroy those they preyed on." What you mean, said the businessman scoffing at his words.

"Among most of the top Army brass was the feeling, after the Tet-Offensive that the Viet Nam war might end up a stale mate like the Korean War. To win a war the perusing army must have an objective? In Viet Nam there was no clear objective because the main focus was put on taking back control of the cities, that became objective No.1. Of course all this was kept secret from the American Public, besides the rest of the world. And it's real simple if you don't fight to keep your house from being taken over then there is no point fighting any place else for anybody else's. The President refused to run for re-election in 1968, because he knew what was getting ready to go down and wanted no parts of it. Not all the Brass wanted to go along with that kind of war, but it was pointed out that the British had to conduct two 'Opium Wars' to subdue, and bring the Chinese people under control, staying that way from the mid-nineteenth century until 1949. The reason that Chairman Moa kicked the Western powers out of China is because his people had been humiliated, abused, and oppressed for so long. The main weapon used against the Chinese was the ingredient from the 'Poppy' grown in the region known as the 'Golden Triangle'. And do you know were the processing and distributing markets are in Laos, Thailand, and Viet Nam. Maybe this is why the French committed half a million troops; they hated to have to give up there 'French Connection'. Then it became the U.S. turn and their only objective was to kill as many of the enemy as they could 'Search and Destroy' to keep from losing not only face but that valuable commodity."

The business man was shaking his head. "You talking about something that happened half way round the world some thirty years ago, what's the point?" Dropping his eyes the old man continued. "Ten years ago in 1989 my old employers the F.B.I. came out with some alarming statistics, 21,000 Americans murdered who lost their lives as a result of violence, most from gun related with 85% being of minority races, sense then the rate has been steadily increasing. Even if the rate stayed the same that would mean 200,000 young American citizens, of which over half were innocent, in the wrong place at the wrong time. In any war it's always the civilians who suffer the most death and destruction. We know there was a war in Viet Nam that claimed over 50, 000 of our service men and women from 1965 to 1975, but we can't close our eyes to what is happing on the streets and the neighborhoods of America. Before the late 1960's and the height of that war 'over there' the gun violence among young people hadn't exploded. It wasn't until the defiance and protest of the war which in the beginning was unexpected then after dragging on and on, had become unwanted, and unpopular, that people began to say enough. At that time the Civil Rights movement was in full swing turning mostly violent and ugly after the death of Dr. King. The fire of rebellion had to be snuffed out, so it came to pass that a tidal wave of drugs sweep across the American landscape, to extinguish the flames. The quest for more drugs brought about the desire for more and greater profits off its sale and with that the need for easier accessible deadly weapons to protect the product, investment, and territory to sell the contraband with the money and stakes going higher along with death rate. All this was the ingrediance for the perfect storm of 'war over here.' It seems the sons and grandsons of those who served during the Viet Nam area are still fighting a war that gets more deadly with the passing of time."

By no means am I excusing the fathers especially the minority fathers who failed at their jobs. All of us must take responsibility for our in-actions. In 1995 we had the 'Million Man March' in which we had all pledged to atone and make amends for the harm we had caused our people, communities, and families. We had come from all over the country, by every means that we could, one of my buddies and I hopped freights, and hitch hiked to get there just to take that pledge with all the others who were there, and commitment ourselves on the mall in front of the U.S. Capitol. Most of us had good attentions when we left Washington D.C. yet when we got back home failed at holding up our end of the bargin. The path way to Hell is paved with good intentions, especially if there aren't any deeds behind them.

Now we are a year away from the turn of the century, and our big cities are either turning into waste lands or battle grounds. One main weapon of our own destruction, what we used to call the old Saturday night special, are as easy for our young people to obtain as toys or candy from the stores. I dread to think what the 21st century has in store. One thing is for sure great Empires like Rome crumbled from within, before the Barbarians stormed the gates, they were dying from the inside, and it seems like we are on the verge of some greatly horrible event that will sweep us all into the obis. Wheatear it be our 'Higher Powers' great tribulation or Man's Armageddon. No man knows the day or hour, but one thing is for certain, as Dr. King once said 'either we learn to live together as brothers or we'll perish as fools." The businessman stood, as he embraced the old man. "God be with you brother." Then he looked up at the stars on this clear night. "Father please be with us all."